WESTMAR COLLEGE LIBRARY

ARISTOTLE

The Great Educators

Edited by NICHOLAS MURRAY BUTLER

ARISTOTLE

AND

ANCIENT EDUCATIONAL IDEALS

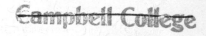
Campbell College

Library No. 2105

BY

THOMAS DAVIDSON

27515

WESTMAR COLLEGE LIBRARY
LE MARS, IOWA

NEW YORK
CHARLES SCRIBNER'S SONS
1899

LA
75
.D24

COPYRIGHT, 1892, BY

CHARLES SCRIBNER'S SONS.

YORK COLLEGE

Library No.

PREFACE

IN undertaking to treat of Aristotle as the expounder of ancient educational ideas, I might, with Kapp's *Aristoteles' Staatspaedagogik* before me, have made my task an easy one. I might simply have presented in an orderly way and with a little commentary, what is to be found on the subject of education in his various works — Politics, Ethics, Rhetoric, Poetics, etc. I had two reasons, however, for not adopting this course: (1) that this work had been done, better than I could do it, in the treatise referred to, and (2) that a mere restatement of what Aristotle says on education would hardly have shown his relation to ancient pedagogy as a whole. I therefore judged it better, by tracing briefly the whole history of Greek education up to Aristotle and down from Aristotle, to show the past which conditioned his theories and the future which was conditioned by them. Only thus, it seemed to me, could his teachings be seen in their proper light. And I have found that this method has many advantages, of which I may mention one. It has enabled me to show the close connection that existed at all times between Greek education and Greek social and political life, and to present the

v

one as the reflection of the other. And this is no small advantage, since it is just from its relation to the whole of life that Greek education derives its chief interest for us. We can never, indeed, return to the purely political education of the Greeks; they themselves had to abandon that, and, since then,

A boundless hope has passed across the earth —

a hope which gives our education a meaning and a scope far wider than any that the State aims at; but in these days, when the State and the institution which embodies that hope are contending for the right to educate, it cannot but aid us in settling their respective claims, to follow the process by which they came to have distinct claims at all, and to see just what these mean. This process, the method which I have followed has, I hope, enabled me, in some degree, to bring into clearness. This, at all events, has been one of my chief aims.

In treating of the details of Greek educational practice, I have been guided by a desire to present only, or mainly, those which contribute to make up the complete picture. For this reason I have omitted all reference to the training for the Olympic and other games, this (so it seems to me) being no essential part of the system.

It would have been easy for me to give my book a learned appearance, by checkering its pages with references to ancient authors, or quotations, in the original, from them; but this has seemed to me both unnecessary and unprofitable in a work intended for the general public. I have, therefore, preferred to place at the heads of the different chapters, in English mostly, such quotations as seemed to express, in the most striking way, the spirit of the different periods and theories of Greek education. Taken together, I believe these quotations will be found to present a fairly definite outline of the whole subject.

In conclusion, I would say that, though I have used a few modern works, such as those of Kapp and Grasberger, I have done so almost solely for the sake of finding references. In regard to every point I believe I have turned to the original sources. If, therefore, my conclusions on certain points differ from those of writers of note who have preceded me, I can only say that I have tried to do my best with the original materials before me. I am far from flattering myself that I have reached the truth in every case, and shall be very grateful for corrections, in whatever spirit they may be offered; but I trust that I have been able to present in their essential features, the "ancient ideals of education."

THOMAS DAVIDSON.

" GLENMORE,"
KEENE, ESSEX CO., N.Y.
October, 1891.

CONTENTS

BOOK I.

INTRODUCTORY.

CHAPTER VI.

BOOK II.

THE HELLENIC PERIOD (B.C. 776-338).

PART I.

THE "OLD EDUCATION" (B.C. 776-480).

CHAPTER I.

CHAPTER II.

CHAPTER III.

CHAPTER IV.

CHAPTER V.

Part II.

THE "NEW EDUCATION" (B.C. 480–338).

CHAPTER I.

CHAPTER II.

CHAPTER III.

BOOK III.

ARISTOTLE (B.C. 384–322).

CHAPTER I.

CHAPTER II.

CHAPTER III.

CHAPTER IV.

CHAPTER V.

CHAPTER VI.

CHAPTER VII.

BOOK IV.

THE HELLENISTIC PERIOD (B.C. 338–A.D. 313).

CHAPTER I.

CHAPTER II.

PAGE

CHAPTER III.

CHAPTER IV.

APPENDIX.

Book I

INTRODUCTORY

ARISTOTLE

CHAPTER I

CHARACTER AND IDEAL OF GREEK EDUCATION

Nothing in excess ! — SOLON.

No citizen has a right to consider himself as belonging to himself; but all ought to regard themselves as belonging to the State, inasmuch as each is a part of the State; and care for the part naturally looks to care for the whole. — ARISTOTLE.

GREEK life, in all its manifestations, was dominated by a single idea, and that an æsthetic one. This idea, which worked sometimes consciously, sometimes unconsciously, was PROPORTION. The Greek term for this (*Logos*) not only came to designate the incarnate Word of Religion, but has also supplied many modern languages with a name for the Science of Manifested Reason — Logic. To the Greek, indeed, Reason always meant ratio, proportion; and a rational life meant to him a life of which all the parts, internal and external, stood to each other in just proportion. Such proportion was threefold; *first*, between the different parts of the individual human being; *second*, between the individual and his fellows in a social whole; *third*, between the human, as such, and the overruling divine. The realization of this threefold harmony in the indi-

3

vidual was called by the Greeks WORTH (Ἀρετή, usually, but incorrectly, rendered Virtue). There has
come down to us, from the pen of Aristotle, in whom
all that was implicit in Hellenism became explicit,
a portion of a pæan addressed to this ideal. It may
be fitly inserted here, in a literal translation.

To WORTH.

O Worth! stern taskmistress of human kind,
Life's noblest prize:
O Virgin! for thy beauty's sake
It is an envied lot in Hellas even to die,
And suffer toils devouring, unassuaged —
So well dost thou direct the spirit
To fruit immortal, better than gold
And parents and soft-eyed sleep.
For thy cause Jove-born Hercules and Leda's sons
Much underwent, by deeds
Thy power proclaiming.
For love of thee Achilles and Ajax to Hades' halls went down.
For thy dear beauty's sake Atarneus' nursling too widowed the
    glances of the sun.
Therefore, as one renowned for deeds and deathless, him the
    Muses shall exalt,
The daughters of Memory, exalting so the glory of Stranger-
    guarding Jove, and the honor of friendship firm.

With regard to this ideal, four things are especially
noteworthy; *first*, that it took an exhaustive survey of
man's nature and relations; *second*, that it called for
strong, persistent, heroic effort; *third*, that it tended to
sink the individual in the social whole and the universal order; *fourth*, that its aim was, on the whole, a
static perfection. The first two were merits; the
second two, demerits. The first merit prevented the

Greeks from pursuing one-sided systems of education; the second, from trying to turn education into a means of amusement. Aristotle says distinctly, "Education ought certainly not to be turned into a means of amusement; for young people are not playing when they are learning, since all learning is accompanied with pain." The first demerit was prejudicial to individual liberty, and therefore obstructive of the highest human development; the second encouraged Utopian dreams, which, being always of static conditions, undisturbed by the toils and throes essential to progress, tend to produce impatience of that slow advance whereby alone man arrives at enduring results. To this tendency we owe such works as Plato's *Republic* and Xenophon's *Education of Cyrus*.

CHAPTER II

BRANCHES OF GREEK EDUCATION

With thee the aged car-borne Peleus sent me on the day whereon from Phthia to Agamemnon he sent thee, a mere boy, not yet acquainted with mutual war or councils, in which men rise to distinction — for this end he sent me forth to teach thee all these things, to be a speaker of words and a doer of deeds. — (*Phœnix in*) HOMER.

Above all and by every means we provide that our citizens shall have good souls and strong bodies. — LUCIAN.

LIFE is the original school — life, domestic and social. All other schools merely exercise functions delegated by the family and by society, and it is not until the latter has reached such a state of complication as to necessitate a division of labor that special schools exist. Among the Homeric Greeks we find no mention of schools, and the only person recorded as having had a tutor is Achilles, who was sent away from home so early in life as to be deprived of that education which he would naturally have received from his father. In what that education consisted, we learn from the first quotation at the head of this chapter. It consisted in such training as would make the pupil "a speaker of words and a doer of deeds" — a man eloquent and persuasive in council, and brave and resolute on the field of battle. For these ends he required, as Lucian says, a good soul and a strong body.

These expressions mark the two great divisions into which Greek education at all periods fell — MENTAL

6

EDUCATION and PHYSICAL EDUCATION — as well as their original aims, viz. goodness (that is, bravery) of soul and strength of body. As time went on, these aims underwent considerable changes, and consequently the means for attaining them considerable modifications and extensions. Physical education aimed more and more at beauty and grace, instead of strength, while mental education, in its effort to extend itself to all the powers of the mind, divided itself into literary and musical education.

As we have seen, the Greeks aimed at developing all the powers of the human being in due proportion and harmony. But, in course of time, they discovered that the human creature comes into the world with his powers, not only undeveloped, but already disordered and inharmonious ; that not only do the germs of manhood require to be carefully watched and tended, but also that the ground in which they are to grow must be cleared from an overgrowth of choking weeds, before education can be undertaken with any hope of success. This clearing process was called by the later Greeks *Katharsis*, or Purgation, and played an ever-increasing part in their pedagogical systems. It was supposed to do for man's emotional nature what Medicine undertook to do for his body. The means employed were mainly music and the kindred arts, which the ancients believed to exert what we should now call a dæmonic effect upon the soul, drawing off the exciting causes of disturbing passion, and leaving it in complete possession of itself. It would hardly be too much to say that the power to exert this purgative influence on the soul was regarded by the ancients

as the chief function and end of the Fine Arts. Such
was certainly Aristotle's opinion.

When purgation and the twofold education of body
and mind had produced their perfect work, the result
was what the Greeks called *Kalokagathia* (καλοκἀγαθία)
that is, Fair-and-Goodness. Either half of this ideal
was named ἀρετή (*aretê*), Worth or Excellence. We
are expressly told by Aristotle (*Categories*, chap.
viii.) that the adjective to ἀρετή is σπουδαῖος (*spou-
daios*), a word which we usually render into English
by "earnest." And we do so with reason; for to the
Greek, Excellence or Worth meant, above all, earnestness, genuineness, truthfulness, thoroughness, absence
of frivolity.

CHAPTER III

CONDITIONS OF EDUCATION

Some hold that men become good by nature, others by training, others by instruction. The part that is due to nature obviously does not depend upon us, but is imparted through certain divine causes to the truly fortunate. — ARISTOTLE.

It is not merely begetting that makes the father, but also the imparting of a noble education. — JOHN CHRYSOSTOM.

There are two sorts of education, the one divine, the other human. The divine is great and strong and easy; the human small and weak and beset with many dangers and delusions. Nevertheless, the latter must be added to the former, if a right result is to be reached. — DION CHRYSOSTOM.

The same thing that we are wont to assert regarding the arts and sciences, may be asserted regarding moral worth, viz. that the production of a completely just character demands three conditions — nature, reason, and habit. By "reason" I mean instruction, by "habit," training. . . . Nature without instruction is blind; instruction without nature, helpless; exercise (training) without both, aimless. — PLUTARCH.

To the realization of their ideal in any individual the Greeks conceived three conditions to be necessary, (1) a noble nature, (2) persistent exercise or training in right action, (3) careful instruction. If any one of these was lacking, the highest result could not be attained.

(1) To be well or nobly born was regarded by the Greeks as one of the best gifts of the gods. Aristotle defines noble birth as "ancient wealth and worth," and this fairly enough expresses the Greek view

9

generally.   Naturally enough, therefore, the Greek
in marrying looked above all things to the chances of
a worthy offspring.   Indeed, it may be fairly said
that the purpose of the Greek in marriage was, not
so much to secure a helpmeet for himself as to find a
worthy mother for his children.   In Greece, as everywhere else in the ancient world, marriage was looked
upon solely as an arrangement for the procreation
and rearing of offspring.   The romantic, pathological
love-element, which plays so important a part in
modern match-making, was almost entirely absent
among the Greeks.   What love there was, assumed
either the noble form of enthusiastic friendship or
the base one of free lust.   In spite of this, and of
the fact that woman was regarded as a means and not
as an end, the relations between Greek husbands and
wives were very often such as to render the family
a school of virtue for the children.   They were noble,
sweet, and strong, — all the more so, it should seem,
that they were based, not upon a delusive sentimen-
tality, but upon reason and a sense of reciprocal duty.

(2) The value of exercise, practice, habituation,
seems to have been far better understood by the ancients than by the moderns.   Whatever a man has to
do, be it speaking, swimming, playing, or fighting, he
can learn only by doing it; this was a universally accepted maxim.   The modern habit of trying to teach
languages and virtues by rules, not preceded by extensive practice, would have seemed to the ancients as
absurd as the notion that a man could learn to swim
before going into the water.   Practice first; theory
afterwards: do the deed, and ye shall know of the

doctrine — so said ancient Wisdom, to which the notion that children should not be called upon to perform any act, or submit to any restriction, without having the grounds thereof explained to them, would have seemed the complete inversion of all scientific method. It was by insisting upon a certain practice in children, on the ground of simple authority, that the ancients sought to inculcate the virtues of reverence for experience and worth, and respect for law.

(3) The work begun by nature, and continued by habit or exercise, was completed and crowned by instruction. This had, according to the Greek, two functions, (*a*) to make action free, by making it rational, (*b*) to make possible an advance to original action. Nature and habit left men thralls, governed by instincts and prescriptions; instruction, revelation of the grounds of action, set them free. Such freedom, based on insight, was to the thinkers of Greece the realization of manhood, or rather, of the divine in man. "The truth shall make you free" — no one understood this better than they. Hence, with all their steady insistence upon practice in education, they never regarded it as the ultimate end, or as any end at all, except when guided by insight, the fruit of instruction. A practicality leading to no widening of the spiritual horizon, to no freeing insight, was to them illiberal, slavish, paltry — "banausic," they said, — degrading both to body and soul.

CHAPTER IV

SUBJECTS FOR EDUCATION

It is right that Greeks should rule over barbarians, but not barbarians over Greeks; for those are slaves, but these are free men. — EURIPIDES.

Barbarian and slave are by nature the same. — ARISTOTLE.

Nature endeavors to make the bodies of freemen and slaves different; the latter strong for necessary use, the former erect and useless for such operations, but useful for political life. . . . It is evident, then, that by nature some men are free, others slaves, and that, in the case of the latter, slavery is both beneficial and just. — *Id.*

Instruction, though it plainly has power to direct and stimulate the generous among the young . . . is as plainly powerless to turn the mass of men to nobility and goodness (*Kalokagathia*). For it is not in their nature to be guided by reverence, but by fear, nor to abstain from low things because they are disgraceful, but (only) because they entail punishment. — *Id.*

IN thinking of Greek education as furnishing a possible model for us moderns, there is one point which it is important to bear in mind: Greek education was intended only for the few, for the wealthy and well-born. Upon all others, upon slaves, barbarians, the working and trading classes, and generally upon all persons spending their lives in pursuit of wealth or any private ends whatsoever, it would have seemed to be thrown away. Even well-born women were generally excluded from most of its benefits. The subjects of education were the sons of full citizens, themselves preparing to be full citizens, and to exercise all the functions of such. The duties of such persons were completely summed up under two heads, duties to the family and duties to the State, or, as the Greeks said, œconomic and political duties. The free citizen not only acknowledged no other duties besides these, but he looked down upon persons who sought occupation in any other sphere. Œconomy and Politics, however, were very comprehensive terms. The former included the three relations of husband to wife, father to children, and master to slaves and property; the latter, three public functions, legislative, administrative, and judiciary. All occupations not included under these six heads the free citizen left to slaves or resident foreigners. Money-making, in the modern sense, he despised, and, if he devoted himself to art or philosophy, he did so only for the benefit of the State. If he improved the patrimony which was the condition of his free citizenship, he did so, not by chaffering or money-lending, but by judicious management, and by kindly, but firm, treatment of his slaves. If he performed any great artistic service to the State — for example, if he wrote a tragedy for a State religious festival (and plays were never written for any other purpose) — the only reward he looked forward to was a crown of olive or laurel and the respect of his fellow-citizens.

The Greeks divided mankind, in all the relations of life, into two distinct classes, a governing and a governed, and considered the former alone as the subject of education; the latter being a mere instrument in its hands. The governing class required education in order that it might govern itself and the other class, in accordance with reason and justice; that other, receiving its guidance from the governing class, required no education, or only such as would enable it to obey. It followed that the duty of the governing class was to govern; of the governed, to obey. Only in this correlation of duties did each class find its usefulness and satisfaction. Any attempt to disturb or invert this correlation was a wilful running in the teeth of the laws of nature, a rebellion against the divine order of things.

As husband, father, master in the family, and as legislator, officer, judge in the State, each member of the governing class found his proper range of activities; and he did wrong, degrading himself to the level of the serving class, if he sought any other. This view, in a more or less conscious form, pervades the whole ancient world, conditioning all its notions and theories of education; and Paul the Apostle only echoed it when he said to wives: "Wives, be in subjection to your own husbands as to the Lord"; to children: "Children, obey your parents in the Lord: for this is right"; and to slaves: "Slaves, be obedient unto them that according to the flesh are your masters with fear and trembling, in singleness of heart, as unto Christ."

CHAPTER V

EDUCATION AS INFLUENCED BY TIME, PLACE, AND CIRCUMSTANCES

The peculiar character of each form of government is what establishes it at the beginning and what usually preserves it. . . . Since the whole State has but one end, it is plainly necessary that there should be one education for all the citizens. — ARISTOTLE.

EDUCATION among the Greeks, as among every other progressive people, varied with times and circumstances. The education of the Homeric Greeks was not that of the Athenians in the days of Aristotle, nor the latter the same as the education of the contemporary Spartans or Thebans. Moreover, the education actually imparted was not the same as that demanded or recommended by philosophers and writers on pedagogics. It is true that the aim was always the same; Worth, Excellence, Fair-and-Goodness (ἀρετή, καλοκἀγαθία); but this was differently conceived and differently striven after at different times and in different places.

Among the Homeric Greeks, as we have seen, education, being purely practical, aiming only at making its subject "a speaker of words and a doer of deeds," was acquired in the actual intercourse and struggles of life. The simple conditions of their existence demanded no other education and, consequently, no special educational institutions. These conditions, as

15

described by Homer, though by no means barbarous,
are primitive. Nomadism has long been left behind
and the later village-communities have been mostly
merged in walled towns, generally situated at some
distance from the shore, on or near a hill, whose summit forms a citadel for refuge in cases of danger.
Even in the most advanced of these towns, however,
the type of civilization is still largely patriarchal.
The government is in the hands of chiefs or kings
(βασιλῆες) claiming to be born and bred of Jove, as,
indeed, in a sense, they were, since they ruled quite as
much by right of personal worth, which more than
anything is due to the grace of God, as by hereditary
title. Worth in those days consisted in physical
strength, courage, beauty, judgment, and power to
address an assembly, and any king proving deficient
in these qualities would soon have found his position
insecure, or been compelled to fortify it by lawless
tyranny. The functions devolving upon the king were
mainly three, those of judge, military commander, and
priest. The first required judgment and ready speech;
the second, strength and intelligent courage; the third,
personal beauty and dignity. Though the kings were
allowed to exercise great power, this was not irre-
sponsible or arbitrary. On the contrary, it was compatible with great public freedom in speech and action.
Slavery existed only to a limited extent and in a mild
form. All free heads of families, however poor, had
a right to attend the popular assembly, which the king
consulted on all important matters, and at which the
freëst discussion was allowed. When the kings exercised judicial power, they did so in accordance with

certain *themistes* or laws, held to have originated with Zeus, and not according to their own caprice. As there was little commerce in those days, the inhabitants of the ancient cities, when not engaged in warfare, devoted themselves chiefly to agriculture, cattle-raising, and the useful arts. In these even the kings thought it no shame to engage. We find Paris helping to build his own palace, Odysseus constructing his own bed, Lycaon cutting wood to make chariot-rails, and so on. Similarly, we find Helen and other princesses spinning and weaving, while Nausicaa, the daughter of the Phæacian king, washes the clothes of the family.

In such a primitive society, unacquainted with letters, the higher education found but few aspirants. The only persons of scientific pretensions mentioned by Homer are the physicians (who are likewise surgeons) and the soothsayers. The former are highly appreciated, and are always chiefs. The soothsayers are the exponents of divine omens to the community, and occupy a kind of official position, like the Hebrew prophets. No artists, strictly speaking, are mentioned by Homer, except the bard, and he is much honored, as historian, teacher, and inspirer. We find, indeed, that Achilles and Paris are proficients in music; but such cases seem exceptional. Of artisans, several are mentioned — the worker in wood, the worker in horn and ivory, the potter (who uses the wheel), and so on. The existence of others is implied — the weaver, the mason, the metal-worker, etc.

If there were no special schools in the heroic age, life was so lived as to be an excellent school. Then, as at all other times, it was extremely social, far more so than our modern life. This was due chiefly to three causes, (1) the smallness of the states, which made it possible for every citizen to know, and to feel his solidarity with, every other, (2) the absence of titles and formalities, which had not yet been introduced from the East, (3) the fact that the people, especially the men, spent the greater part of the day in the open air, — in the streets and agora, — and so were continually rubbing against each other. This sociality had much to do with the shaping of the Greek character, the salient elements of which are thus enumerated by Zeller, the historian of Greek philosophy: "A strong sense of freedom, combined with a rare susceptibility to proportion, form, and order, a keen relish for companionship in life and action, a social tendency which compelled the individual to combine with others, to submit to the general will, to follow the traditions of his family and his community."

Between the simple social condition described by Homer and that for which Aristotle wrote, there intervened a period of at least six hundred years. During that time many great changes took place in the social and political life of the Greeks, demanding corresponding changes in education. These changes were due to several causes, (1) the natural human tendency toward freedom, (2) the influence of foreign nations, (3) the development of commerce, (4) the introduction of letters, (5) the rise of philosophy, (6) the Persian Wars. Though all these are closely interwoven with each other, there can be no harm in treating them separately.

(1) The tendency toward freedom, so essentially characteristic of human nature, was especially so of the nature of the Greeks. Among them it rapidly manifested itself in an ordered series of political forms, beginning with patriarchalism, and ending variously in the various states and races. There is, indeed, hardly a single form of political life that was not realized among the Greeks at some time or place. It was this that made it possible for Aristotle to write a work on Politics which, in the words of a recent political writer, "has remained for two thousand years one of the purest sources of political wisdom."

The varied and changeful political life of the Greeks was in itself a great education. It made them aware of the principles, political and ethical, upon which society rests, and rendered necessary a faculty of clear and ready expression, which reacted most favorably upon their intellectual and æsthetic faculties. It was in the school of practical politics that the Greeks acquired their rhetoric; and Aristotle, in his treatise on Poetry, tells us that, while "the older poets made their characters talk like statesmen, the later ones made theirs talk like rhetoricians." Not only, indeed, did political life react upon the drama, but, in developing rhetoric, it drew attention to language and led to the sciences of grammar and logic, both of which were thus called into existence by real social needs (see p. 102).

(2) Greece, lying, as it did, between three continents, and in the thoroughfare of the ancient nations, could hardly fail to be visited by many different races, or, considering its beauty and commercial advantages,

to be coveted by them. From this followed two consequences, (*a*) that the Greeks were a very mixed race, (*b*) that they were, from the first and at all times, in manifold contact with foreign peoples. That they were a mixed race, is attested alike by their language, their mythology, and their legends. That they were in close and continual communication with foreign peoples, is rendered evident by their alphabet, their art, and the direct statements of their historians. Although it is true that the Greeks, especially after the Persian Wars, regarded themselves as a superior and chosen people, calling all others "barbarians," and considering them as fit only to be slaves, it is not the less true that hardly one of all the arts and sciences which they ultimately carried to a high degree of perfection had its origin in Greece proper. All appear first in the colonies settled among "barbarians," — in Egypt, Asia Minor, Thrace, Crete, Sicily, or Italy. Architecture, sculpture, painting, poetry — epic, lyric, dramatic — music, history, politics, philosophy, were all borrowed, transformed, and, with the exception perhaps of tragedy and painting, carried to a high degree of excellence in the colonies, before they were transplanted to the mother-country. It is beyond any doubt that even the Homeric legends are of "barbarian" origin, though from what people they were borrowed is uncertain. It was the plasticity and versatility of their character, due in part to their mixed blood, that, by enabling them to appropriate and assimilate the arts and sciences of their neighbors, raised the Greeks to a new plane of civilization and made them the initiators of a new epoch in history, the epoch of life according to reason. Sir Henry Sumner Maine says, "Except the blind forces of Nature, nothing moves in this world which is not Greek in its origin."

(3) It was chiefly through commerce that the arts and sciences borrowed by the colonial Greeks found their way into Greece proper. That foreign art-objects were introduced into it at an early period, is rendered certain by the recent discoveries at Mycenæ, Sparta, and other places, as well as by statements in the Homeric poems. That these were followed later by artists, bringing with them foreign art-processes and appliances, is equally certain. The earliest sculptors whose names are known to us, Dipœnus and Scyllis, were natives of Crete, settled in Sicyon; and the earliest poetic guild of which we have any mention is that of the Homeridæ in the island of Chios. But, besides introducing art and artists into Greece, commerce tended to educate the Greeks in other ways. It made them acquainted with foreign manners and luxuries, and forced them to learn the arts of navigation, ship-building and exchange, which again rendered necessary an acquaintance with arithmetic and the art of writing. And this leads us to

(4) The Introduction of Letters. This event, the date of which is uncertain, not only exercised a most furthering influence on the arts and sciences, but gave rise to a new branch of education. Letters were probably first used for diplomatic and trade purposes, then for inscriptions, and last of all for the perpetuation of literary productions. So much of a change did they effect in Greek education that even in the best times

the whole of the literary and scientific education was called simply "letters" (γράμματα). As late as the time of Plato letters seem to have been considered a part of Music, and to have been taught by the same teacher as the latter; but Aristotle already distinguishes the two. It is extremely probable that the introduction of letters was the immediate cause of the establishment of schools for youth; for we find no mention of them prior to that event.

(5) The introduction of letters was closely followed by the rise of Philosophy, or the reflective spirit. Up to about the year 600 B.C., the Greeks, like the rest of the world, lived by habit, tradition, and prescription, handed on, with little or no criticism, from generation to generation. Their ideal world was shaped by the works of Homer and Hesiod. "Hesiod is the teacher of most," says Heraclitus. About the date named, however, society having advanced to a condition of organization which made possible a leisure class, there begins to appear a new spirit, destined to revolutionize, not only Greece, but the whole world. Armed with a *what?* a *which?* a *why?* and a *wherefore?* it no longer blindly accepts the world of nature and man, but calls upon it to give an account of itself. Science, philosophy, and art are the result.

At first the new spirit turns to nature with a *what?*; but, gradually discovering that the answer to this brings no complete explanation of the world, it propounds its other questions. It thus arrives at a consciousness of four distinguishable elements in the constitution of things, — four causes (αἴτια, αἰτίαι), as they were termed, — (1) matter, (2) form, (3) efficiency,

(4) end or aim. At the same time, and by the same process, it is forced to a recognition of the presence of reason (λόγος) and intelligence (νοῦς) in the world, since form, efficiency, and aim all presuppose both. It is thus compelled to turn from nature to man, and man's mind, as the highest known expression of reason and intelligence, and to devote itself to the consideration of spirit, as alone promising any true explanation of the world. The process is a slow and difficult one, and the history of it is the history of Greek science, philosophy, and art.

Before the rise of philosophy, the teacher of the people had been the rhapsode, or public reciter; after that event he gradually gives place to the sophist (σοφιστής, one who makes wise), or, as he later with more modesty calls himself, the philosopher (φιλόσοφος, lover of wisdom). The history of Greece for centuries is, on its inner side, a history of the struggle between what the rhapsode represents and what the philosopher represents, between popular tradition and common sense on the one hand, and individual opinion and philosophy on the other. The transition from the first to the second of these mental conditions was accomplished for the world, once for all, by the Greeks, and the turning-point in the process is marked by

(6) The Persian Wars (B.C. 490–479). The victories gained in these at Marathon, Salamis, and Platææ, victories the most brilliant that history records, exerted a most powerful influence upon the thought and life of the Greeks. The consciousness of having, with their small numbers, over and over again, both by land and by sea, discomfited and crushed the

countless hosts of an empire which for generations had threatened their peace and liberty, made them at once feel the superiority of their own characters and civil institutions to those of the Persians, and draw a clear line of demarcation between Greek and barbarian. From this point on, they felt themselves to be a chosen people, a nation destined by the gods to rule all others. "The soul of Greece had conquered the bulk of Persia." Persia was bulk and body; Greece was soul and spirit. This conviction appears at once in all the departments of Greek life. In the sphere of art we may instance the *Prometheia* of Æschylus and the Parthenon. In the former, what does the conflict between Zeus and Prometheus mean but the conflict between Greek spirituality, intellect, and freedom, on the one hand, and barbarian materiality, instinct, and thraldom or necessity, on the other? And what is the latter but a matchless pæan in stone to Divine Wisdom, as the conqueror of brute force? In the sphere of thought, we find Parmenides, Anaxagoras and, above all, Socrates (born ten years after the second Persian War), turning consciously to the study of spirit. "To be and to think are the same thing," says the first of these: "All things were confused; then Mind came and reduced them to order," says the second; "Know thyself" is the chosen motto of the third. In the political sphere we find the Athenians trying to make the State an instrument of intelligence and virtue, and insisting upon education as a means thereto. Other and less desirable results followed from the Persian Wars; but these can be better stated and estimated in another connection.

Such were the chief causes that contributed to transform the simple patriarchal State of the Homeric Greeks, with its purely practical education at home and in the field, into the free polity of the Greeks of the days of Miltiades, Themistocles, and Æschylus, with its complicated institutions and manifold education. It has seemed better to enumerate these causes than to try to trace the steps of the transformation itself. Indeed this would have been a hopeless task, owing to the lack of historical data.

CHAPTER VI

EPOCHS IN GREEK EDUCATION

When they (our ancestors) began to enjoy leisure for thought, as the result of easy circumstances, and to cherish more exalted ideas with respect to worth, and especially when, in the period before and after the Persian Wars, they came to entertain a high opinion of themselves, on account of their achievements, they pursued all kinds of education, making no distinction, but beating about generally. — ARISTOTLE.

IN treating of Greek education subsequent to the introduction of letters and the establishment of schools, we shall be obliged, in the interest of clearness, to make three distinctions: —

(1) Between the educational systems of different periods.

(2) Between the educational systems of different peoples and states.

(3) Between the education actually imparted in the various states, and that recommended by theorists or philosophers.

In pursuance of the first, it will be convenient first to distinguish two main periods, the Hellenic, and the Hellenistic, and then to subdivide these into minor periods.

I. *The Hellenic Period* (776–338 B.C.). This includes, roughly speaking, the whole historic life of free Greece, from the date of the first Olympiad to that of the absorption of Greece into the Macedonian Empire. It naturally subdivides itself into two periods, (a) 776–450; (b) 450–338.

(a) That of the "Old Education," authoritative and puritanical, whose aim was the training of good citizens, god-fearing, law-abiding, patriotic, and brave.

(b) That of the "New Education," rationalistic and "liberal," whose aim was the training of formidable individuals, self-centred, law-despising, time-serving, and cunning.

It is in the struggle between the two systems, and in the practical triumph of the latter, that Greece loses her moral fibre; so that her citizens, weakened through sundering selfishness, fall an easy prey to the foreign invader.

II. *The Hellenistic Period* (338 B.C.–313 A.D.). This extends from the Battle of Chæronea, in which Greece lost her independence, to the definitive triumph of Christianity, which brought a new ideal and a new spirit into life and education. It naturally subdivides itself into two periods, (a) B.C. 338–146; (b) B.C. 146–A.D. 313.

(a) The Macedonian Period, during which Macedonian influence prevailed, and Greek thought and education, absorbing foreign, chiefly Oriental, elements, tended toward an encyclopædic cosmopolitanism. During this period, Alexandria is the centre of Greek influence.

(b) The Roman Period, during which, as Horace says, "Captive Greece took captive her rude conqueror," and Rome became, alongside Alexandria, a diffusive centre of Greek thought, art, and education.

Between the two great periods, the Hellenic and the Hellenistic, stands the man who draws up the testament of the former and outlines the programme of the latter, the Macedonian Greek, ARISTOTLE.

Our second distinction will lead us to treat separately, in the Hellenic period, the educational system of the three Greek races, (1) the Æolic, (2) the Doric, (3) the Ionic, the first having its chief centre at Thebes, the second at Sparta, the third at Athens. For an account of the education of the first our data are but meagre; with the main features of Spartan and Athenian education we are well acquainted. In education, as in everything, Sparta was conservative, socialistic, and aristocratic, while Athens tended to liberalism, individualism, and democracy. Hence Sparta clung desperately to the "Old Education," and almost closed her doors against art, letters, and philosophy, while Athens, dragged into the "New Education," became the home of all these. It must always be borne in mind that, in favoring individualism and the "New Education," Athens was abandoning the Hellenic ideal, and paving the way for the cosmopolitanism of the Hellenistic period. In this latter, we shall have to distinguish between the educational systems of Athens, Alexandria, and Rome.

Our third distinction is that between individual theory and popular practice. In all epochs of their history the Greek states produced men who strove to realize in thought and imagination the ideal of their people, and to exhibit it as an aim, an encouragement, and an inspiration, in contrast with the imperfect actual. In more than one case this ideal modified the education of the following periods. Of course, such theories did not arise until practice was compelled to defend itself by producing sanctions, either in religion or in reason, and it may perhaps be affirmed that the aim of them all was to discover such sanctions for the Greek ideal. Among the many educational theorists of Greece, there are six who especially deserve to be considered: (1) Pythagoras, who in Southern Italy sought to graft on the Doric ideal a half-mystical, half-ethical theology, and a mathematical theory of the physical world; (2) Xenophon, who sought to secure the same ideal by connecting it with a monarchical form of government; (3) Plato, who sought to elevate it, and find a sanction for it in his theory of super-sensuous ideas; (4) ARISTOTLE, who presented in all its fulness the Hellenic ideal, and sought to find sanctions for it in history, social well-being, and the promise of a higher life; (5) Quintilian, who, in Rome, embodies the rhetorical or worldly education of the Hellenistic period; and (6) Plotinus, who presents an ideal of philosophical or other-worldly education, and paves the way for the triumph of Christian dogma.

Book II

THE HELLENIC PERIOD (B.C. 776–338)

PART I

THE "OLD EDUCATION" (B.C. 776–480)

CHAPTER I

EDUCATION FOR WORK AND FOR LEISURE

When we consider the different arts that have been discovered, and distinguish between those which relate to the necessary conditions of life and those which contribute to the free enjoyment of it (διαγωγή), we always consider the man who is acquainted with the latter wiser than him who is acquainted with the former, for the reason that the sciences of the latter have no reference to use. Hence it was only when all the necessary conditions of life had been attained that those arts were discovered which have no reference either to pleasure or to the common needs of life; and this took place first in those countries where men enjoyed leisure. — ARISTOTLE.

The free life of God is such as are our brief best moments. — *Id.*

It is not fitting that the free enjoyment of life should be permitted to boys or to young persons; for the crown of perfection belongs not to the imperfect. — *Id.*

Obviously, the free enjoyment of life demands not only the noble but also the pleasant; for happiness consists of these too. — *Id.*

AMONG the Homeric Greeks, whose life was almost entirely devoted to practical pursuits, education was mainly practical, aiming to produce "a speaker of words and a doer of deeds." As civilization advanced, and higher political forms were evolved, certain classes

33

of men found themselves blessed with leisure which they were not inclined to devote to mere play. In order to make a worthy use of this leisure, they required a certain training in those arts which were regarded as befitting a free man. Education, accordingly, in some states, widened its scope, to include those accomplishments, which enable men to fill their hours of freedom with refined and gracious enjoyment — music and letters. Music, indeed, had been cultivated long before, not only by professional bards, but even by princes, like Achilles and Paris; this, however, was for the sake of amusement and recreation rather than of the free enjoyment of life. It had been regarded as a means, not as an end. We must be careful, in our study of Greek life and education, not to confound play and recreation, which are for the sake of work, with the free enjoyment of life, which is an end in itself, and to which all work is but a means. "Enjoyment is the end." We shall see, as we proceed, to what momentous results this distinction leads, how it governs not only all education but all the institutions of life, and how it finally contributes to break up the whole civilization which it determines. It may fairly be said that Greece perished because she placed the end of life in individual æsthetic enjoyment, possible only for a few and regarding only the few.

In historic Greece, music came to be an essential part of the education of every free man. Even free women learnt it. Along with music went poetry, and when this came to be written down, it was termed "letters." As every free man came to be his own

minstrel and his own rhapsode, the professional minstrel and rhapsode disappeared, and the Homeric
poems even, in order to be preserved from oblivion,
were committed to writing by an enlightened tyrant
— Pisistratus.

The first portion of the Greek people that attained
a degree of civilization demanding an education for
hours of leisure, was the Æolian race, and particularly
the Asiatic portion of it.   Accordingly we find that
all the earliest musicians and poets, didactic and lyric,
are Æolians — Hesiod, Terpander, Arion, Alcæus,
Sappho, Pittacus, etc.   Lesbos seems to have taken
the lead in this "higher education."   The last five
names all belong to that island, which produced also
the earliest Greek historian and prose-writer — Hel-
lanicus.   But the Æolians, though earliest in the
field, were soon outstripped by the other two races, the
Doric and the Ionic.   Æolian education and culture
never advanced beyond music and lyric poetry.   It
knew no drama, science, or philosophy.

The Æolians were followed, almost simultaneously,
by the Dorians and Ionians, who pursued two widely
divergent directions.   The former borrowed the lyric
education and culture of the Æolians, and produced
several lyric poets of distinguished merit — Tyrtæus,
Alcman, Ibycus, Stesichorus: nay, they even advanced
far enough to take the first steps in science, philosophy, and dramatic poetry.   Pythagoras, Epicharmus,
Sophron, Xenarchus, and Susarion were all Dorians.
But the progress of the race was retarded and finally
checked by rigid political institutions of a socialistic
character, which, by suppressing individual initiative,
reduced the whole to immobility.

The Ionians, on the contrary, borrowing freely from both Æolians and Dorians, and evolving ever freer and freer institutions, carried education and culture to a point which has never been passed, and rarely, if ever, reached, in the history of our race. And when they ceased to grow, and decay set in, this was due to exactly the opposite cause to that which stunted them among the Dorians; namely, to excessive individualism, misnamed liberty. Individualism ruined Athens.

Although education assumed different forms among different portions of the Greek race, there are certain features that seem to have been common to all these forms during the epoch of the "Old Education." Two of these deserve attention.

First. Education was everywhere a branch of statecraft, and the State itself was only the highest educational institution. This was equally true whether the schools were public, as at Sparta, or private, as at Athens. Everywhere citizenship was a degree, conferred only upon sons of free citizens, after a satisfactory examination (δοκιμασία).

Second. The stages or grades of education were everywhere the same, although their limits were not everywhere marked by the same number of years. The first, extending usually from birth to the end of the seventh year, was that of home education; the second, extending from the beginning of the eighth year to the end of the sixteenth or, perhaps oftener, the eighteenth year, was that of school education; the third, extending from the beginning of the seventeenth or nineteenth year to the end of the twentieth (in Sparta of the thirtieth), was that of college education, or education for the duties of citizenship; the fourth, including the remainder of life, was that of university education, or education through the State, which then was the only university. At the beginning of the third period, the young men took their first State examination, and if they passed it successfully, they received the degree of Cadet or Citizen-novice (ἔφηβος); but it was only at the beginning of the fourth period, and after they had passed a second examination (δοκιμασία εἰς ἄνδρας), that they received the degree of Man and Citizen and were permitted to exercise all the functions of freemen. The State then became, in a very real sense, their *Alma Mater*.

In most states, this graded education fell only to the lot of males, the education of females stopping short with the first grade, the family, which was regarded as their only sphere. It was otherwise at Sparta, Teos, and apparently among the Æolians generally. As a consequence it is only among the Æolians and Dorians that any poetesses of note appear — Sappho, Corinna, Telesilla, etc. Although, however, woman's sphere was the family, and she was considered to have done her duty when she worthily filled the place of wife, mother, and mistress, there was nothing to prevent her from acquiring the higher education, if she chose to do so. That she did not often so choose, seems true; still there are examples of learned women even among the Athenians. The daughter of Thucydides is said to have continued his history after his death, and, whether the statement be true or not, the fact that it was made shows that the ability to write history was not regarded as impossible or surprising in a woman.

CHAPTER II

ÆOLIAN OR THEBAN EDUCATION

Hesiod is the teacher of most. — HERACLITUS.

When thou art dead, thou shalt lie in the earth.
Not even the memory of thee shall be
Thenceforward nor forever; for thou hast
No share in the Pierian roses; but
Ev'n in the halls of Hades thou shalt flit,
A frightened shadow, with the shadowy dead.
— SAPPHO (*to an uneducated woman*).

What rustic hoyden ever charms the soul,
That round her ankles cannot kilt her coats?— *Id.*

THE Æolians appear to have been the earliest of the Greek races to make any considerable advance in culture. Their claim to Homer can hardly be sustained; but they certainly produced Hesiod, most of the greater lyric poets and poetesses, and the first historian. For a time they bade fair to lead the culture of Greece. But the promise was not fulfilled. During the palmy period of Greek history, they were not only the most uncultured and uncouth of the Greeks, but they even prided themselves upon their boorishness of speech and manner, and derided culture. In the glorious struggle in which Greece maintained the cause of culture and freedom against Persia, Thebes, then the chief centre of Æolianism, sided with the barbarian, as, indeed, was natural.

38

Theban education was, of course, a reflex of the character of the Theban and, indeed, of the Bœotian, people. Its main divisions were those of Greek education generally, — Gymnastics and Music; but the former was learnt solely for athletic purposes, and the latter mainly for use at banquets and drinking-bouts, in which the Bœotians found their chief delight. Letters were studied as little as at Sparta (see p. 47), and the language of the people remained harsh and unmusical. Of higher education there was hardly a trace. The sophists passed Bœotia by. Even Pindar, who was by birth a Theban, and a sincerely patriotic one, sought and found recognition anywhere rather than among his own people. He did not even write in their dialect.

The reason for this backwardness on the part of the Bœotian Æolians lay in the fact that they lived, as a conquering race, in the midst of a people superior to them in every respect save strength, and could maintain their ascendency only by brute force. When this failed, and the conquered race, which had never forgotten Cadmus and its ancient traditions, came to the front, education and culture found their way even to Thebes. It was due to this change in political conditions that a Pindar could arise, and it was doubtless the demand for culture consequent thereupon that induced certain members of the scattered Pythagorean school (see p. 54) to seek refuge in Thebes and there devote themselves to teaching. Among these were Philolaus [1] and Lysis, the latter of whom was proba-

---

[1] It is worth while to note that it was a passage from Philolaus that suggested to Copernicus the revolution of the earth round a centre.

bly the author of the famous "Golden Words" (see p. 57). But he has a better claim to fame than this; for he was the teacher of the bravest and most lovable man that Greece ever produced — Epaminondas.

If any enthusiastic believer in the power of education desire to fortify his cause by means of a brilliant example, he will find none superior to Epaminondas; for there can hardly be any question that it was the earnest, systematic, religious, and moral Pythagorean training which he received from the aged Lysis, whom he treated as a father, that made him what he was, and enabled him to do what he did, — which was nothing less than to place Thebes at the head of Greece. Thebes rose and fell with Epaminondas. But that was not all. It was the example of Epaminondas that kindled the ambition of Philip of Macedon, who was educated under his eye, and of his far more famous son, Alexander, who made all Greece a province of his empire. Pythagoras, Lysis, Epaminondas, Philip, Alexander — in five brief generations an earnest teacher conquers a world!

From the time of Epaminondas on, Thebes followed the ordinary course of Greek education.

CHAPTER III

DORIAN OR SPARTAN EDUCATION

Go, tell at Sparta, thou that passest by,
That here, obedient to her laws, we lie.
— SIMONIDES (*Epitaph on the Three Hundred
who fell at Thermopylæ*).

This is a matter for which the Lacedæmonians deserve approbation: they are extremely solicitous about the education of their youth and make it a public function. — ARISTOTLE.

The Lacedæmonians impart to their children the look of wild beasts, through the severity of the exercises to which they subject them, their notion being that such training is especially calculated to heighten courage. — *Id*.

These are so far behind in education and philosophy that they do not learn even letters. — ISOCRATES.

OLD MEN. We *were* once strong men (youths).
MEN. And we *are ;* if you will, behold.
BOYS. And we *shall be* far superior. — *Spartan Choric Anthem.*

They asked no clarion's voice to fire
    Their souls with an impulse high :
But the Dorian reed and the Spartan lyre
    For the sons of liberty!
So moved they calmly to their field,
    Thence never to return,
Save bearing back the Spartan shield,
    Or on it proudly borne ! — HEMANS.

There was a law that the cadets should present themselves naked in public before the ephors every ten days ; and, if they were well knit and strong, and looked as if they had been carved and hammered into shape by gymnastics, they were praised ; but if their limbs showed any flabbiness or softness, any little swelling or sus-

41

picion of adipose matter due to laziness, they were flogged and justiced there and then. The ephors, moreover, subjected their clothing every day to a strict examination, to see that everything was up to the mark. No cooks were permitted in Lacedæmon but flesh-cooks. A cook who knew anything else was driven out of Sparta, as physic for invalids. — ÆLIAN.

EVERY rational system of education is determined by some aim or ideal more or less consciously set up. That of the Dorians, and particularly of the Spartans, may be expressed in one word — STRENGTH, which, in the individual, took the form of physical endurance, in the State, that of self-sufficiency (αὐτάρκεια). A self-sufficient State, furnishing a field for all the activities and aspirations of all its citizens, and demanding their strongest and most devoted exertions — such is the Dorian ideal. It is easy to see what virtues Dorian education would seek to develop — physical strength, bravery, and obedience to the laws of the State. Among the Dorians the human being is entirely absorbed in the citizen. The State is all in all.

The Dorian ideal realized itself chiefly in two places, Crete and Sparta. Both these were repeatedly held up in ancient times as models of well-governed states, and even Plato puts the substance of his *Laws* into the mouth of a Cretan.

About the details of Cretan education we are but poorly informed. Two things, however, we know: (1) that Lycurgus, the reputed founder of Spartan education, was held to have drawn many of his ideas from Crete, and (2) that the final result of Cretan education — and the same is true of all education that merges the man in the citizen — was, in spite of its

strictness, demoralizing.   The character of the people
was summed up by their poet Epimenides, a contemporary of Solon's, in a famous line quoted by St. Paul,
"The Cretans are always liars, evil beasts, lazy
bellies."

With regard to Spartan education our information
is much greater, and we may therefore select it as the
type of Dorian education generally.

The Peloponnesian Dorians having, through contact
with the more civilized peoples whom they conquered,
lost much of that rigorous discipline and unquestion-
ing loyalty which made them formidable, were, in the
ninth century B.C., becoming disorganized, so that in
two of the Dorian states they were assimilated by
the native population, the Argives and the Messe-
nians.   The same process was rapidly going on in the
third state, Lacedæmon, when Lycurgus, fired with
patriotic zeal, resolved to put an end to it, by restor-
ing among his people the old Dorian military discipline.   To prepare himself for this task, he visited
Crete and studied its institutions.   On his return he
persuaded his countrymen to submit to a "Constitution," which ever afterwards went by his name.   This
constitution included a scheme of education, whose
aim was a thorough training of the whole of the free
citizens, both male and female, (1) in physical endurance, and (2) in complete subordination to the State.
The former was sought to be imparted by means of a
rigorous and often cruel, system of gymnastics; the
latter, through choric music and dancing, including
military drill.   Spartan education, therefore, was
confined to two branches, Gymnastics and Music.

Instruction in letters was confined to the merest elements. Sparta accordingly never produced a poet, an historian, an artist, or a philosopher of any note. Even the arrangers of her choruses were foreigners — Tyrtæus, Terpander, Arion, Alcman, Thaletas, Stesichorus.

As Spartan education was nothing more or less than a training for Spartan citizenship, we must preface our account of it by a few words on the Spartan State.

The government of Sparta was in the hands of a closed aristocracy, whose sole aim was the maintenance of its own supremacy, as against (1) foreign enemies, (2) *Perioikoi*, or disfranchised native citizens, (3) Helots, or native serfs. To secure this, it formed itself into a standing army, with a strict military organization. Sparta, its one abode, was a camp; all free inhabitants were soldiers. Though they were compelled to marry, the city contained no homes. The men and, from the close of their seventh year, the boys, lived in barracks and ate at public tables (*Phiditia*). The women had but one recognized function, that of furnishing the State with citizens, and were educated solely with a view to this. No other virtue was expected of them. Aristotle tells us that "they lived in every kind of profligacy and in luxury." Polyandry was common, and, when a woman lost all her husbands, she was often compelled to enter into relations with slaves, in order that she might not fail in her political duty.

Among a people organized on the basis of brute force, it were vain to look for any of the finer traits of human nature — gentleness, tenderness, sympathy, pity, mercy. The mercilessness and cruelty of the Spartans were proverbial. Perioikoi and Helots incurring the displeasure or suspicion of the authorities were secretly put to death, without even the form of a trial. A striking instance of such cruelty is recorded by Thucydides. The facts are thus stated by Grote (*History of Greece*, vol. ii, pp. 376–7): "It was in the eighth year of the Peloponnesian War, after the Helots had been called upon for signal military efforts in various ways, . . . that the ephors felt especially apprehensive of an outbreak. Anxious to single out the most forward and daring Helots, as men from whom they had most to dread, they issued proclamation that every member of that class who had rendered distinguished services should make his claim known at Sparta, promising liberty to the most deserving. A large number of Helots came forward to claim the boon: not less than two thousand of them were approved, formally manumitted, and led in solemn procession round the temples, with garlands on their heads, as an inauguration to their coming life of freedom. But the treacherous garland only marked them out as victims for sacrifice: every man of them forthwith disappeared; the manner of their death was an untold mystery."

Spartan education was entirely conducted by the State, at the expense of the State, and for the ends of the State. It differed in this respect from nearly every other system of Greek education. It was divided into four periods, corresponding respectively to childhood, boyhood, youth, and manhood.

(*a*) CHILDHOOD. — As soon as the Spartan child

came into the world, the State, through officers ap pointed for that purpose, sent to examine it. If it seemed vigorous, and showed no bodily defect, it was permitted to live, and forthwith adopted by the State; otherwise it was carried to the mountains and thrown over a precipice. The children accepted by the State were for the next seven years left in charge of their mothers, but, doubtless, still under State surveillance. Just how they were trained during these years, we do not know. We can only guess that they under- went very much the same process as other Greek chil- dren, any difference being in the direction of rigor. As the details of Greek education generally will be dealt with under the head of Athens, they may be omitted here.

(b) BOYHOOD. — On completing his seventh year, the Spartan boy was transferred from his mother's house and care to a public barracks and the direct tuition of the State. Although the boys were in charge of a special officer (παιδονόμος), who divided them into squads and companies, and arranged their exercises for them, they were nevertheless taught to regard every grown man as a teacher, and every such man was expected to correct them promptly and rigorously, whenever he saw them doing wrong. At the same time, every boy was expected to form an intimate con- nection with some one man, who then, to a large extent, became responsible for his conduct; and, though the choice in this matter rested with the parties concerned, it was considered a disgrace in a man, no less than in a boy, to be without such connection. Though this arrangement, it is said, often led to lamentable abuses, there can be no doubt that it admirably served the purposes of Sparta. It furnished every boy with a tutor, who, under the circumstances, could hardly fail to treat him kindly, and who was interested in making him surpass all other boys in courage and endurance. This friendly influence of teacher on pupil was something in which the Greeks at all times strongly believed, and which formed an important force in all their education. In Sparta, as in Crete and Thebes, it was legally recognized. One of the duties of Spartan "inspirer" (εἰσπνήλας or εἴσπνηλος), as he was called, was to teach his young friend (ἀΐτας) to demean himself properly on all occasions, and to hold his tongue except when he had something very important to say. In this way it was that the young Spartans received their moral education, and acquired that effective brevity of speech which to this day we call "laconic."

The formal education of Spartan boys consisted mainly of gymnastics, music, choric dancing, and larceny. Their literary education was confined to a little reading, writing, and finger-arithmetic; everything beyond this was proscribed. And the reasons for this proscription are not difficult to discover. Sparta staked everything upon her political strength, and this involved two things, (1) equality among her free citizens, and (2) absolute devotion on their part to her interest, both of which the higher education would have rendered impossible. Education establishes among men distinctions of worth quite other than military, and gives them individual interests distinct from those of the State. It was the same reason that induced Rome, during the best period of her history, to exclude her citizens from all higher education, which is essentially individual and cosmopolitan.

The education of the Spartan boys was conducted mostly in the open air and in public, so that they were continually exposed to the cheers or scoffs of critical spectators, to whom their performances were a continual amusement of the nature of a cock-fight. Whether the different "inspirers" betted on their own boys may be doubtful; but they certainly used every effort to make them win in any and every contest, and the "inspirer" of a "winning" boy was an envied man. The result was that many boys lost their lives amid cheers, rather than incur the disgrace of being beaten. Inasmuch as the sole purpose of gymnastics was strength and endurance; of dancing, order; and of music, martial inspiration, it is easy to see what forms these studies necessarily assumed; and we need only stop to remark that Dorian music received the unqualified approbation of all the great educational writers of antiquity, — even of Aristotle, who had only words of condemnation for Spartan gymnastics.

There was only one branch of Spartan school-education that was not conducted in public, and that was larceny. The purpose of this curious discipline was to enable its subjects to act, on occasion, as detectives and assassins among the ever discontented and rebellious Helots. How successful it was, may be judged from the incident recorded on page 45. Larceny, when successfully carried out under difficult circumstances, was applauded; when discovered, it was severely punished. A story is told of a boy who, rather than betray himself, allowed a stolen fox, concealed under his clothes, to eat out his entrails.

In one respect Spartan education may claim superiority over that of most other Greek states: it was not confined to one sex. Spartan girls, though apparently permitted to live at home, were subjected to a course of training differing from that of their brothers only in being less severe. They had their own exercise-grounds, on which they learnt to leap, run, cast the javelin, throw the discus, play ball, wrestle, dance, and sing; and there is good evidence to show that their exercises had an admirable effect upon their physical constitution. That the breezy daughters of Sparta were handsomer and more attractive than the hot-house maidens of Athens, is a well-attested fact. Many Spartan women continued their athletic and musical exercises into ripe womanhood, learning even to ride spirited horses and drive chariots. If we may believe Aristotle, however, the effect of all this training upon their moral nature was anything but desirable. They were neither virtuous nor brave.

(c) YOUTH. — About the age of eighteen, Spartan boys passed into the class of *epheboi*, or cadets, and began their professional training for war. This was their business for the next twelve years, and no light business it was. For the first two years they were called *melleirenes*, and devoted themselves to learning the use of arms, and to light skirmishing. They were under the charge of special officers called *bideoi*, but had to undergo a rigid examination before the ephors every ten days (see p. 41). Their endurance was put to severe tests. Speaking of the altar of Artemis Orthia, Pausanias says: "An oracle commanded the people to imbrue the altar with human blood, and hence arose the custom of sacrificing on it a man chosen by lot. Lycurgus did away with this practice, and ordained that, instead, the cadets should be scourged before the altar, and thus the altar is covered with blood. While this is going on, a priestess stands by, holding, in her arms the wooden image (of Artemis). This image, being small, is, under ordinary circumstances, light; but, if at any time the scourgers deal too lightly with any youth, on account of his beauty or his rank, then the image becomes so heavy that the priestess cannot support it; whereupon she reproves the scourgers, and declares that she is burdened on their account. Thus the image that came from the sacrifices in the Crimea has always continued to enjoy human blood." This Artemis appears, with a bundle of twigs in her arm, next to Ares, among the Spartan divinities, on the frieze of the Parthenon. At twenty years of age, the young men became *eirenes*, and entered upon a course of study closely resembling actual warfare. They lived on the coarsest food, slept on reeds, and rarely bathed or walked. They exercised themselves in heavy arms, in shooting, riding, swimming, ball-playing, and in conflicts of the most brutal kind. They took part in complicated and exhausting dances, the most famous of which was the Pyrrhic, danced under arms. They manned fortresses, assassinated Helots, and, in cases of need, even took the field against an enemy.

(d) MANHOOD. — At the age of thirty, being supposed to have reached their majority, they fell into the ranks of full citizens, and took their share in all political functions. They were compelled to marry, but were allowed to visit their wives only rarely and by stealth. They sometimes had two or three children before they had ever seen their wives by daylight. When not engaged in actual war, they spent much of their time in watching the exercises of their juniors, and the rest in hunting wild boars and similar game in the mountains. Like Xenophon, they thought hunting the nearest approach to war.

Such was the education that Sparta gave her sons. That it produced strong warriors and patriotic citizens, there can be no doubt. But that is all: it produced no men. It was greatly admired by men like Xenophon and Plato, who were sick of Athenian democracy; but Aristotle estimated it at its true worth. He says: "As long as the Laconians were the only people who devoted themselves to violent exercises, they were superior to all others; but now they are inferior even in gymnastic contests and in war. Their former superiority, indeed, was not due to their training their young men in this way, but to the fact that they alone did so." And even Xenophon, at the end of a long panegyric on the Spartan constitution, is obliged to admit that already in his time it has fallen from its old worth into feebleness and corruption, and this in spite of the fact that he had his own sons educated at Sparta. When Sparta fell before the heroic and cultured Epaminondas, she fell unpitied, leaving to the world little or nothing but a warning example.

CHAPTER IV

PYTHAGORAS

Virtue and health and all good and God are a harmony. — PY-THAGORAS.

One is the principle of all. — PHILOLAUS the Pythagorean.

All things that are known have number. — *Id.*

The principles of all virtue are three, knowledge, power, and choice. Knowledge is like sight, whereby we contemplate and judge things; power is like bodily strength, whereby we endure and adhere to things; choice is like hands to the soul, whereby we stretch out and lay hold of things. — THEAGES the Pythagorean.

THE Doric discipline, even in Sparta, where it could exhibit its character most freely, produced merely soldiers and not free citizens or cultivated men. It was, nevertheless, in its essential features, the Hellenic ideal, and numerous attempts were made to remedy its defects and to give it permanence, by connecting it with higher than mere local and aristocratic interests. One of the earliest and most noteworthy of these was made by Pythagoras.

This extraordinary personage appears to have been born in the island of Samos in the first quarter of the sixth century B.C. Though he was born among Ionians, his family appears to have been Achaian and, to some extent, Pelasgian (Tyrrhenian), having emigrated from Phlius in the Argolid. After distinguishing himself in Ionia, he emigrated in middle life to

Magna Græcia, and took up his abode in the Achaian colony of Croton, then a rich and flourishing city. The cause of his emigration seems to have been the tyranny of Polycrates, which apparently imparted to him a prejudice against Ionic tendencies in general. Whether he derived any part of his famous learning from visits to Egypt, Phœnicia, Babylonia, etc., as was asserted in later times, is not clear. It is not improbable that he visited Egypt, and there is good reason for believing that he became acquainted with Phœnician theology through Pherecydes of Syros. That he was an omnivorous student is attested by his contemporary, Heraclitus. He was undoubtedly affected by the physical theories current in his time in Ionia, while he plainly drew his political and ethical ideas from Sparta or Crete.

Of his activity in Ionia we know little; but we may perhaps conclude that it was of the same nature as that which he afterwards displayed in Italy. Here he appeared in the triple capacity of theologian, ethical teacher, and scientist. His chief interest for us lies in the fact that he was apparently the first man in Greece, and, indeed, in the western world, who sought to establish an ethical institution apart from the State. In this respect he bears a strong resemblance to the prophet Isaiah, who may be said to have originated the idea of a Church (see p. 133). Pythagoras' aim seems to have been to gather round him a body of disciples who should endeavor to lead a perfect life, based upon certain theological or metaphysical notions, and guided by a rule of almost monastic strictness. Like other men who have found themselves in the

midst of irreverence, selfishness, and democratic vulgarity and anarchy, he believed that his time demanded moral discipline, based upon respect for
authority and character, with a firm belief in future
retribution, and inculcated by a careful study of the
order and harmony of nature; and such discipline he
strove, with all his might, to impart. Having no
faith in the capacity of the State to be an instrument
for his purpose, he set to work independently of it,
and seems to have met with very marked success,
drawing to him many of the best men and women of
Southern Italy. So numerous and powerful, indeed,
did his followers become that they held the balance
of power in several cities, and were able to use it for
the enforcement of their own principles. As these
were exceedingly undemocratic, and opposed to the
tendencies of the time, they finally roused bitter
opposition, so that the Pythagoreans were persecuted
and attempts made to exterminate them with fire
and sword. In this way their political influence was
broken, and their assemblies suppressed; but the
effect of Pythagoras' teaching was not lost. His
followers, scattered abroad throughout the Hellenic
world, carried his precepts and his life-ideal with
them. In the following centuries they found many
noble sympathizers — Pindar, Socrates, Plato, Epicharmus, etc. — and underwent many modifications,
until they finally witnessed a resurrection, in the
forms of Neo-Pythagoreanism and Neo-Platonism,
after the Christian era. In these later guises, Pythagoreanism lost itself in mysticism and contemplation,
turning its followers into inactive ascetics; but in its

original form it seems to have been especially adapted to produce men of vigorous action and far-sighted practicality. Milo of Croton, the inimitable wrestler; Archytas of Tarentum, philosopher, mathematician, musician, inventor, engineer, general, statesman; and Epaminondas, the greatest and noblest of Theban generals, were professed Pythagoreans.

We might perhaps express the aim of Pythagoras' pedagogical efforts by the one word HARMONY. Just as he found harmony everywhere in the physical world, so he strove to introduce the same into the constitution of the human individual, and into the relations of individuals with each other. He may perhaps be regarded as the originator of that view of the world, of men, and of society which makes all good consist in order and proportion, a view which recommends itself strongly to idealists, and has given birth to all those social Utopias, whose static perfection seems to relieve the individual from the burden of responsibility, and which have been dangled before the eyes of struggling humanity from his days to ours. According to this view, which had its roots in Greek thought generally, the aim of education is to find for each individual his true place and to make him efficient therein. Man is made for order, and not order for man. He is born into a world of order, as is shown by the fact that number and proportion are found in everything that is known. Pythagoras, in his enthusiasm for his principle, carried his doctrine of numbers to absurd lengths, identifying them with real things; but this enthusiasm was not without its valuable results, since it is to Pythagoras and his school that we owe the sciences of geometry and music. Moreover, experience must have taught him that it is one thing to propound a theory, another to make it effective in regulating human relations. In order to accomplish the latter object, he invoked the aid of divine authority and of the doctrines of metempsychosis and future retribution. Hence his educational system had a strong religious cast, which showed itself even outwardly in the dignified demeanor and quiet self-possession of his followers.

Harmony, then, to be attained by discipline, under religious sanctions, was the aim of Pythagoras' teaching. Believing, however, that only a limited number of persons were capable of such harmony, he selected his pupils with great care, and subjected them to a long novitiate, in which silence, self-examination, and absolute obedience played a prominent part. The aim of this was to enable them to overcome impulse, concentrate attention, and develop reverence, reflection, and thoughtfulness, the first conditions of all moral and intellectual excellence. While the first care was directed to their spiritual part, their bodies were by no means forgotten. Food, clothing, and exercise were all carefully regulated on hygienic and moral principles.

Regarding the details of Pythagoras' educational system we are not well informed; but the spirit and tendency of it have been embalmed for us in the so-called *Golden Words*, which, if not due to the pen of Pythagoras himself, certainly reach back to very near his time, and contain nothing at variance with what we otherwise know of his teaching. We insert a literal version.

The Golden Words.

The Gods immortal, as by law disposed,
First venerate, and reverence the oath:
Then to the noble heroes, and the powers
Beneath the earth, do homage with just rites.

Thy parents honor and thy nearest kin,
And from the rest choose friends on virtue's scale.
To gentle words and kindly deeds give way,
Nor hate thy friend for any slight offence.
Bear all thou canst; for Can dwells nigh to Must.
These things thus know.

                        What follow learn to rule:
The belly first, then sleep and lust and wrath.
Do nothing base with others or alone:
But most of all thyself in reverence hold.

Then practise justice both in deed and word,
Nor let thyself wax thoughtless about aught:
But know that death's the common lot of all.

Be not untimely wasteful of thy wealth,
Like vulgar men, nor yet illiberal.
In all things moderation answers best.

Do things that profit thee: think ere thou act.

Let never sleep thy drowsy eyelids greet,
Till thou hast pondered each act of the day:
" Wherein have I transgressed?   What have I done?
What duty shunned?"—beginning from the first,
Unto the last.   Then grieve and fear for what
Was basely done; but in the good rejoice.

These things perform; these meditate; these love.
These in the path of godlike excellence
Will place thee, yea, by Him who gave our souls
The number Four, perennial nature's spring!
But, ere thou act, crave from the gods success.

These precepts having mastered, thou shalt know
The system of the never-dying gods
And dying men, and how from all the rest
Each thing is sunder'd, and how held in one :
And thou shalt know, as it is right thou shouldst,
That nature everywhere is uniform,
And so shalt neither hope for things that lie
Beyond all hope, nor fail of any truth.

But from such food abstain as we have named,
And, while thou seek'st to purge and free thy soul,
Use judgment, and reflect on everything,
Setting o'er all best Thought as charioteer.

Be glad to gather goods, nor less to lose.

Of human ills that spring from spirit-powers
Endure thy part nor peevishly complain.
Cure what thou canst : 'tis well, and then reflect :
"Fate never lays too much upon the good."

Words many, brave and base, assail men's ears.
Let these not disconcert or trammel thee ;
But when untruth is spoken, meekly yield.

What next I say in every act observe :
Let none by word or deed prevail on thee
To do or say what were not best for thee.
Think ere thou act, lest foolish things be done ; —
For thoughtless deeds and words the caitiff mark ; —
But strongly do what will not bring regret.
Do naught thou dost not know ; but duly learn.
So shall thy life with happiness o'erflow.

Be not neglectful of thy body's health ;
But measure use in drink, food, exercise —
I mean by ' measure ' what brings no distress.

Follow a cleanly, simple mode of life,
And guard against such acts as envy breed.

Then, if, when thou the body leav'st, thou mount
To the free ether, deathless shalt thou be,
A god immortal, — mortal never more !

In this system six things are noteworthy: (1) Its comprehensiveness, in that it takes account of man's whole nature, — body, soul, and spirit; affections, intellect, and will, and of all his relations — to gods and men, to self and nature: (2) Its aimfulness, in that it promises happiness here and blessedness here- after, as the reward of right living: (3) Its piety, in that it everywhere recognizes the need of divine assist- ance: (4) Its appreciation of science, as insight into the nature and grounds of multiplicity and unity: (5) Its stress laid on right doing, as the condition of right knowing: (6) Its belief in man's divinity and perfec- tibility. It is curious that the poem contains no reference to the doctrine of metempsychosis, which might apparently have been appealed to as a power- ful moral sanction.

That a system like that of Pythagoras, combining the religious, the mystical, the scientific, the ethical, and the social tendencies of the Hellenic mind, should have exerted a deep and abiding influence, need not surprise us. We find profound traces of it, not only in all subsequent Greek thought, but even in foreign systems, such as Essenism, whose elements were Hebrew Naziritism and Greek Pythagoreanism. The relations between Essenism and Christianity have not yet been determined. Of the effect of Pythagoras' teaching on Epaminondas I have already spoken.

CHAPTER V

IONIAN OR ATHENIAN EDUCATION

Let me now give an account of the Old Education, when I, uttering words of justice, was in my prime, and self-control was held in respect. In the first place, a child was not allowed to be heard uttering a grumble. Then all the boys of the quarter were obliged to march in a body, in an orderly way and with the scantest of clothing, along the streets to the music master's, and this they did even if it snowed like barley-groats. Then they were set to rehearse a song, without compressing their thighs, — either " Pallas, mighty city-stormer," or " A shout sounding far," putting energy into the melody which their fathers handed down. And, if any one attempted any fooling, or any of those trills like the difficult inflexions *a la* Phrynis now in vogue, he received a good threshing for his pains, as having insulted the Muses. Again, at the physical trainer's, the boys, while sitting, were obliged to keep their legs in front of them. . . . And at dinner they were not allowed to pick out the best radish-head, or to snatch away anise or celery from their elders, or to gourmandize on fish and field-fares, or to sit with their legs crossed. . . . Take courage, young man, and choose me, the Better Reason, and you shall know how to hate the public square, to avoid the bath-houses, to be ashamed of what is shameful, to show temper when any one addresses you in ribald language, to rise from your seat when your elders approach, and not to be a lubber to your own parents, or to do any other unseemly thing to mar the image of Modesty, or to rush to the house of the dancing-girl, and, while you are gaping at her performances, get struck with an apple by a wench and fall from your fair fame, or to talk back to your father, or, addressing him as Japhet, to revile the old age which made the nest for you. . . . Then, fresh and blooming, you will spend your time in the gymnasia, and not go about the public square, mouthing monstrous jokes, like the young men of to-day, or getting dragged into slippery, gumshon-bamboozling disputes, but, going down to the Academy, with some worthy companion of

60

your own age, you will start a running-match, crowned with white reed, smelling of smilax, leisure and deciduous white poplar, rejoicing in the spring, when the plane-tree whispers to the maple. If you do the things which I enjoin, and give your mind to them, you will always have a well-developed chest, a clear complexion, broad shoulders, and a short tongue. — ARISTOPHANES, *Clouds* (*Speech of Right Reason*).

In their systems of education, some states strive to impart a courageous habit to their people from their very childhood by a painful and laborious training, whereas we, though living in a free and natural way, are ready to meet them in a fair field with no favor. — PERICLES' *Funeral Oration* (*Thucydides*).

I will never disgrace these sacred arms, nor desert my companion in the ranks. I will fight for temples and public property, both alone and with many. I will transmit my fatherland, not only not less, but greater and better, than it was transmitted to me. I will obey the magistrates who may at any time be in power. I will observe both the existing laws and those which the people may unanimously hereafter make, and, if any person seek to annul the laws or to set them at nought, I will do my best to prevent him, and will defend them both alone and with many (all?). I will honor the religion of my fathers. And I call to witness Aglauros, Enyalios, Ares, Zeus, Thallo, Auxo, and Hegemone. — *Oath of the Athenian Epheboi.*

Consider, Men of Athens, what careful provision was made by Solon, the ancient lawgiver, by Draco, and other lawgivers of that period, for the cultivation of good morals. In the first place, they made laws to secure a moral education for our children, and laid down, in plain terms, just what the free-born boy should study and how he should be nurtured ; secondly, they made regulations regarding young men ; and, thirdly, with regard to the other periods of life in their order, including both private persons and public speakers ; and, having recorded these laws, they left them in your keeping, appointing you their guardians. — ÆSCHINES (*against Timarchus*).

IF systems of education are to be classified according to their results — and these are perhaps the fairest test — then the " Old Education " of Athens must be assigned a very high place. The character which she displayed, and the exploits which she performed, in the early decades of the fifth century B.C., bear unequivocal testimony to the value of the training to which her citizens had previously been subjected. This training could perhaps hardly be better characterized than by the word "puritanical." The men who fought at Marathon, Salamis, and Platææ were puritans, trained, in a hard school, to fear the gods, to respect the laws, their neighbors, and themselves, to reverence the wisdom of experience, to despise comfort and vice, and to do honest work. They were not enfeebled by æsthetic culture, paralyzed by abstract thinking, or hardened by professional training. They were educated to be men, friends, and citizens, not to be mere thinkers, critics, soldiers, or money-makers. It was against a small band of such men that the hosts of Persia fought in vain.

It is natural that this "Old Education" of Athens should have a special interest for us, inasmuch as it seems, in great measure, to have solved the problem that must be uppermost with every true educator and friend of education, viz. How can strong, wise, and good men be produced? For this reason, as also because we are the better informed regarding the educational system of Athens than that of any other Greek state, it seems proper to devote special attention to it, treating it as preëminently Greek education. Indeed, whatever is permanently valuable in Greek education is to be found in that of Athens, other systems having mainly but an historical interest for us.

In comparing the education of Athens with that of Sparta, we are at once struck with two great distinctions: (1) While Spartan education is public, Athenian education is mainly private; (2) While Sparta educates for war, Athens educates for peace. As to the former of these, it is not a little remarkable that, while many of the first thinkers of Greece, including Plato and Aristotle, advocated an entirely public education, Athens never adopted it, or even took any steps in that direction. It seems as if the Athenians felt instinctively that socialistic education, by relieving parents of the responsibility of providing for the education of their own children, was removing a strong moral influence, undermining the family, and jeopardizing liberty. Perhaps the example of Sparta was not without its influence. No liberty-loving people, such as the Athenians were, would consent to merge the family in the State, or to sacrifice private life to public order. As to the second distinction, which was all-pervasive, it divides the two peoples by an impassable gulf and assigns them to two different grades of civilizaton. And it was one of which both peoples were entirely conscious. While Sparta represented her ideal by a chained Ares, Athens found hers in a Wingless Victory, a form of Athena, the divinity of political and industrial wisdom. As the aim of Sparta was strength, so that of Athens was WISDOM — the wise man in the wise state. By the "wise man," was meant he whose entire faculties of body, soul, and mind were proportionately and coördinately developed; by the "wise state," that in which each class of the population performed its proper function, and occupied its proper relation toward the rest, and this without any excessive exercise of author-

ity. If the Spartan, like the artificially tamed barbarian, submitted to living by rule and command, the
Athenian, like the naturally civilized man, delighted
to live in a free and natural way (ἀνειμένως διαιτᾶσθαι)
governed from within, and not from without. To
make possible such life was the aim of Athenian education, which, instead of seeking to merge the man
in the State, or to rend the two asunder, treated them
as necessary correlates and strove to balance their
claims.

The endeavor on the part of Athens to steer a middle course between socialism and individualism, is
manifest in the fact that, though she had no public system of education, she took great care to see that her
citizens were thoroughly educated in the spirit of her
institutions, and, indeed, made such education a condition of citizenship, which was thus an academic degree,
conferred only after careful examination. By a law
of Solon's, parents who had failed to give their sons
a proper education lost all claim upon them for support in their old age. Furthermore, Athens subjected
all her male citizens to a systematic preparation for
civil and military functions, before she allowed them
to exercise these.

Athenian education comprised four grades corresponding to four institutions, (1) the family, (2) the
school, (3) the gymnasium or college, (4) the State.
We may consider these in their order.

(1) FAMILY EDUCATION.

The birth of a child was regarded by the Athenians
as a joyful event, as something calling for gratitude

to the gods. This expressed itself in a family festival, called the Amphidromia, celebrated usually on the seventh day after the birth. On this occasion, the child was carried rapidly round the family altar and received its name. A sacrifice was then offered to the gods, the mother was purified, and christening presents were displayed. The child was now a member of the family and under the protection of its gods. For the next seven years, it was wholly in the hands of parents and nurses, the latter being usually slaves. During this time its body was the chief object of care, and everything seems to have been done to render it healthy and hardy. Cradles do not seem to have been in use, and the child was sung to sleep on the nurse's knee. While it was being weaned, it was fed on milk and soft food sweetened with honey. As soon as it was able to move about and direct attention to external objects, it received playthings, such as rattles, dolls of clay or wax, hobby-horses, etc., and was allowed to roll and dig in the sand. Such were the simple gymnastics of this early period. As to the other branch of education, it consisted mostly in being sung to and in listening to stories about gods and heroes, monsters and robbers, of which Greek mythology was full. By means of these the child's imagination was roused and developed, and certain æsthetic, ethical, and national prepossessions awakened. Though children were often frightened from certain acts and habits by threats of bogies coming to carry them off, yet the chief ethical agency employed was evidently strict discipline. To secure good behavior in his children was the first care of the Athenian parent.

Though disinclined to harshness, he never doubted that "he who spareth the rod hateth the child." Children were never placed upon exhibition or applauded for their precocious or irreverent sayings. They were kept as much as possible out of the way of older people, and, when necessity brought them into the presence of these, they were taught to behave themselves quietly and modestly. No Greek author has preserved for us a collection of the smart sayings or roguish doings of Athenian children.

Though the Kindergarten did not exist in those old days, yet its place was, in great measure, filled by the numerous games in which the children engaged, in part at least under their nurses' superintendence. Games played so important a part in the whole life of the Greek people, and especially of the Athenians, that their importance in the education of children was fully recognized and much attention devoted to them. During play, character both displays itself more fully, and is more easily and deeply affected, than at any other time; and, since the whole of the waking life of the child in its earliest years is devoted to play, this is the time when character is formed, and therefore the time which calls for most sedulous care. In playing games, children not only exercise their bodies and their wits; they also learn to act with fairness, and come to feel something of the joy that arises from companionship and friendly rivalry in a common occupation. Moreover, as games have no end beyond themselves, they are admirable exercises in free, disinterested activity and a protection against selfish and sordid habits. Of all this the Athenians were fully aware.

There are probably few games played by children in our day that were not known in ancient Athens. It seems, however, that games were there conducted with more system, and a deeper sense of their pedagogical value, than they are with us. We hear of running, leaping, hopping, catching, hitting, and throwing games, gymnastic games, and games of chance. The ball, the top, the hoop, the swing, the see-saw, the skipping rope, the knuckle-bones were as much in use in ancient, as in modern, times. Cards, of course, there were not; and, indeed, games of chance, though well known, seem rarely to have been indulged in by children. It hardly seems necessary to remark that there were some games peculiar to boys and others to girls, and that the latter were less rude than the former. Doubtless, too, the games played in the city, where the children would have few chances of going beyond their homes, were different from those played in the country, where almost complete freedom to roam in the open air was enjoyed. We must always bear in mind that well-to-do Athenian families spent the greater part of the year at their country-houses, which, with few exceptions, were so near the city that they could be reached even on foot in a single day. This country life had a marked effect upon the education of Athenian children.

(2) School Education.

About the age of seven, the Athenian boy, after being entered on the roll of prospective citizens in the temple of Apollo Patroös, and made a member of a

phratria, went to school, or, rather, he went to two
schools, that of the music-master, and that of the
physical trainer. He was always accompanied thither
and back by a *pedagogue*, who was usually a slave,
who carried his writing-materials, his lyre, etc. (there
being no school-books to carry), and whom he was
expected implicitly to obey. The boys of each
quarter of the city collected every morning at some
appointed place and walked to school, like little soldiers, in rank and file. They wore next to no clothing, even in the coldest weather, and were obliged to
conduct themselves very demurely in the streets.
The school hours were very long, beginning early in
the morning and continuing till late in the evening.
Solon found it necessary to introduce a law forbidding
schoolmasters to have their schools open before sun-
rise or after sunset. It thus appears that boys, after
the age of seven, spent their whole day at school, and
were thus early withdrawn from the influence of their
mothers and sisters, a fact which was not without
its bearing upon morals.

There are several interesting points in connection
with Athenian school life about which our information is so scanty that we are left in some doubt
respecting them. For example, though it is quite
plain that Athens had no system of public instruction,
it is not so clear that she did not own the school
buildings. Again, it is not certain whether music
(including letters) and gymnastics were, or were not,
taught in the same locality. Thirdly, there is some
doubt about the number and order of the hours devoted to each of the two branches of study. In regard

to these points I can state only what seems to me most probable.

As to school buildings, we are expressly told by the author of the fragmentary tract on *The Athenian State*, currently attributed to Xenophon, but probably written as early as B.C. 424, that "the people (δῆμος) builds itself many palæstras, dressing-rooms, baths, and the masses have more enjoyment of these than the few that are well-to-do." If we assume that some of these palæstras were for boys, as we apparently have a right to do, we must conclude that some, at least, if not all, of the schools for bodily training were public edifices, let out by the State to teachers. Like all the great gymnasia, some, and possibly all, of them were situated outside the city walls and had gardens attached to them. Whether the music-schools were so likewise, is doubtful, and this brings us to our second question — whether the two branches of education were taught in the same place. That they were not taught in the same room, or by the same person, is clear enough; but it does not follow from this that they were not taught in the same building, or at any rate in the same enclosed space. Though there seems to be no explicit statement in any ancient author on this point, I think there are sufficient reasons for concluding that, generally at least, they were so taught. If we find that Antisthenes, Plato, and Aristotle, who may be said to have introduced a systematic "higher education" into Athens, opened their schools in the great public gymnasia, frequented by youths and men, we may surely conclude that the lower mental education was not separated from the physical. In the *Lysis* of Plato, we find some young men coming out of a palæstra outside the city walls, and inviting Socrates to enter, telling him that their occupation (διατριβή) consists *mostly* in discussions (τὰ πολλὰ ἐν λόγοις), and that their teacher is a certain Miccus, an admirer of his. Socrates recognizes the man as a capable "sophist," a term never used of physical trainers. On entering, Socrates finds a number of boys and youths (νεανίσκοι) playing together, the former having just finished a sacrifice. It seems to follow directly from this that intellectual education was imparted in the palæstras. If this be true, we may, I think, conclude that in Athens the schools generally were outside the city walls, though the case was certainly different in some other cities.

In regard to our third question, it is clear that, if boys spent their whole day in one place, it would be more easy to divide it profitably between musical instruction and gymnastics than if they spent one part of it in one place, and another in another. Just how it was divided, we do not know, and I have little doubt that much depended upon the notions of parents and the tendencies of different periods. It is quite clear, from certain complaints of Aristotle's, that in Athens parents enjoyed great liberty in this matter. In any case, since, as we know, the institutions of education were open all day, it seems more than probable that one class of boys took their gymnastic lesson at one hour, another at another, and so with other branches of study. It cannot be that the physical training-schools were deserted when the music-schools were in session. I think there is sufficient reason for believing that, generally, the younger boys took their physical exercises in the morning, and their intellectual instruction in the afternoon, the order being reversed in the case of the older boys. How much of the time spent at school was given up to lessons and how much to play, is not at all clear; but I am inclined to think that the playtime was at least as long as the worktime. The schools were for boys what the agora and the gymnasium were for grown men — the place where their lives were spent.

Before we consider separately the two divisions of Athenian education, a few facts common to them may be mentioned. In the first place, they had a common end, which was, to produce men independent but respectful, freedom-loving but law-abiding, healthy in mind and body, clear in thought, ready in action, and devoted to their families, their fatherland, and their gods. Contrary to the practice of the Romans, the Athenians sought to prepare their sons for independent citizenship at as early an age as possible. In the second place, the motives employed in both divisions were the same, viz. fear of punishment and hope of reward. As we have seen, the Athenian boy, if he behaved badly, was not spared the rod. As an offset against this, when he did well, he received unstinted praise, not to speak of more substantial things. Education, like everything else in Greece, took the form of competition. The Homeric line (*Il.*, vi, 208; xi, 784),

" See that thou ever be best, and above all others distinguished,"

was the motto of the Athenian in everything. In
the third place, in both divisions the chief aim was
the realization of capacity, not the furthering of
acquisition. Mere learning and execution were almost
universally despised in the old time, while intelligence and capacity were universally admired. In
the fourth place, in both divisions the utmost care
was directed to the conduct of the pupils, so that
it might be gentle, dignified, and rational. In the
fifth place, education in both its branches was intended to enable men to occupy worthily and soci-
ably their leisure time, quite as much as to prepare
them for what might be called their practical duties
in family, society, and State. The fine arts, according to the Greeks, furnished the proper amusements
for educated men (πεπαιδευμένοι).

(a) Musical (and Literary) Instruction.

Though the Greek word *music* (μουσική) came in
later times to have an extended meaning, in the epoch
of which we are treating, it included only music in
our sense, and poetry, two things which were not
then separated. Aristophanes, as late as B.C. 422, can
still count upon an audience ready to laugh at the
idea of giving instruction in astronomy and geometry,
as things too remote from human interests (*Clouds*,
vv 220 sqq.). The poetry consisted chiefly of the
epics of Homer and Hesiod, the elegiacs of Tyrtæus,
Solon, Theognis, etc., the iambics of Archilochus,
Simonides, etc., and the songs of the numerous lyr-
ists, Terpander, Arion, Alcæus, Alcman, Sappho,
Simonides, etc.   The music was simple, meant to

"sweeten" (ἡδύνειν) the words and bring out their meaning. In fact, the music and the poetry were always composed together, so that the poet was necessarily also a musician. What we call "harmony" was unknown in Greek music at all times, and instrumental music was almost entirely confined to solo-playing.

In treating of Athenian, and, indeed, of all Greek, education, it is of the utmost importance to realize that the intellectual and moral part of it has music and poetry for its starting-point. This is the core round which everything else gathers; this is what determines its character, influence, and ideal. Culture, as distinguished from nature, is the material of Athenian intellectual and moral education; and by this is meant, not the history or theory of culture, as it might be set forth in prose, but culture itself, as embodied in the ideals and forms of music-wedded poetry, appealing to the emotions that stir the will, as well as to the intelligence that guides it.

By making the works of the great poets of the Greek people the material of their education, the Athenians attained a variety of objects difficult of attainment by any other one means. The fact is, the ancient poetry of Greece, with its finished form, its heroic tales and characters, its accounts of peoples far removed in time and space, its manliness and pathos, its directness and simplicity, its piety and wisdom, its respect for law and order, combined with its admiration for personal initiative and worth, furnished, in the hands of a careful and genial teacher, a material for a complete education such as could not well be

matched even in our own day. What instruction in
ethics, politics, social life, and manly bearing could
not find a fitting vehicle in the Homeric poems, not
to speak of the geography, the grammar, the literary
criticism, and the history which the comprehension of
them involved? Into what a wholesome, unsentimen-
tal, free world did these poems introduce the imagina-
tive Greek boy! What splendid ideals of manhood and
womanhood did they hold up for his admiration and
imitation! From Hesiod he would learn all that he
needed to know about his gods and their relation to
him and his people. From the elegiac poets he would
derive a fund of political and social wisdom, and an
impetus to partiotism, which would go far to make
him a good man and a good citizen. From the iambic
poets he would learn to express with energy his
indignation at meanness, feebleness, wrong, and
tyranny, while from the lyric poets he would learn
the language suitable to every genial feeling and
impulse of the human heart. And in reciting or singing all these, how would his power of terse, idiomatic
expression, his sense of poetic beauty and his ear for
rhythm and music be developed! With what a treas-
ure of examples of every virtue and vice, and with
what a fund of epigrammatic expression would his
memory be furnished! How familiar he would be
with the character and ideals of his nation, how deeply
in sympathy with them! And all this was possible
even before the introduction of letters. With this
event a new era in education begins. The boy now
not only learns and declaims his Homer, and sings his
Simonides or Sappho, he learns also to write down

their verses from dictation, and so at once to read and
to write. This, indeed, was the way in which these
two (to us) fundamental arts were acquired. As soon
as the boy could trace with his finger in sand, or
scratch with a stylus on wax, the forms of the letters,
and combine them into syllables and words, he began
to write poetry from his master's dictation. The
writing-lesson of to-day was the reading, recitation,
or singing-lesson of to-morrow. Every boy made his
own reading-book, and, if he found it illegible, and
stumbled in reading, he had only himself to blame.
The Greeks, and especially the Athenians, laid the
greatest stress upon reading well, reciting well, and
singing well, and the youth who could not do all the
three was looked upon as uncultured. Nor could he
hide his want of culture, since young men were continually called upon, both at home and at more or less
public gatherings, to perform their part in the social
entertainment.

The strictly musical instruction of this period was
almost entirely confined to simple, strong Doric airs,
sung to an accompaniment which was played on an
instrument closely resembling the modern guitar (λύρα,
κίθαρις). Complicated and wind instruments were
unpopular, and the softer or more thrilling kinds of
music, Lydian, Phrygian, etc., had not yet been
introduced, at least into schools. Anything like the
skill and execution demanded of professional players,
who were usually slaves or foreigners, was considered
altogether unworthy of a free man and a citizen, and
was therefore not aimed at. Fond as the Athenians
were of the fine arts, they always held professional

skill in any of them, except poetry and musical composition, to be incompatible with that dignity and
virtue which they demanded of the free citizen. A
respectable Athenian would no more have allowed his
son to be a professional musician than he would have
allowed him to be a professional acrobat.

It is difficult for us to understand the way in which
the Greeks regarded music. Inferior as their music
was to ours in all technical ways, it exerted an influence upon their lives of which we can form but a faint
conception. To them it was a dæmonic power, capable of rousing or assuaging the passions, and hence of
being used for infinite good or evil. No wonder, then,
that in their education they sought to employ those
kinds which tended to "purgation" (κάθαρσις), and
to avoid those that were exciting, sentimental, or
effeminate! No wonder that they disapproved of
divorcing music from the intellectual element contained in the words, and allowing it to degenerate
into a mere emotional or sensual luxury! Music the
Greeks regarded, not indeed as a moral force (a
phrase that to them, who regarded morality as a matter of the will, would have conveyed no meaning), but
as a force whose office it was, by purging and harmonizing the human being, to make him a fit subject for
moral instruction. Music, they held, brought harmony, first into the human being himself, by putting
an end to the conflict between his passions and his
intelligent will, and then, as a consequence, into his
relations with his fellows. Harmony within was held
to be the condition of harmony without.

In the period of which I am speaking, no distinction was yet made between music and literature (γράμματα), both being taught by the *citharist* (κιθαριστής). Indeed, the term for teacher of literature (γραμματιστής) was not then invented. But the citharist not only taught literature: he also taught the elements of arithmetic, a matter of no small difficulty, considering the clumsy notation then in use. This was done by means of pebbles, a box of sand, or an abacus similar in principle to that now used by billiard players to keep count of their strokes.

As to the schoolrooms in ancient Athens, they were apparently simple in the extreme; indeed, rather porches open to sun and wind than rooms in the modern sense. They contained little or no furniture. The boys sat upon the ground or upon low benches, like steps (βάθρα), while the teacher occupied a high chair (θρόνος). The benches were washed, apparently every day, with sponges. The only decorations permitted in the schoolrooms, it seems, were statues or statuettes of the Muses and Apollo, and the school festivals or exhibitions were regarded as festivals in honor of these. Indeed, in Greece every sort of festival was regarded as an act of worship to some divinity. The chief school festival seems to have been the *Musēa* (μουσεῖα), at which the boys recited and sang.

(β) *Gymnastics or Bodily Training.*

Under the term *Gymnastics* (γυμναστική), the Greeks generally included everything relating to the culture of the body. The ends which the Athenians sought to reach through this branch of education were health, strength, adroitness, ease, self-possession, and firm, dignified bearing. A certain number of boys, intending to take part in the Olympic and other great games, were allowed to train as athletes under a gymnast (γυμναστής, ἀλείπτης) in the public gymnasia, and under the direction of the State; but these were exceptions. The athlete was not an ideal person at Athens, as he was at Thebes and Sparta.

Gymnastic exercises were conducted partly in the palæstras, or wrestling schools, partly on the race-courses, both of which were under the direction of professional trainers (παιδοτρίβαι). In early times, the palæstra and race-course were simply an open space covered with sand and probably connected with the school (διδασκαλεῖον), thus corresponding to our playground. Later, this space was partly covered over and furnished with dressing-rooms, a bath, seats for spectators, an altar for sacrifices, statues, etc. Of the five gymnastic exercises in which boys were trained, all except wrestling seem to have been conducted on the race-course, so that the palæstra was reserved for what its name implied. It is by no neans certain that every palæstra had a race-course connected with it, at least in the time of which we are speaking, and possibly in many cases the boys took part of their exercises in the public race-course running from the agora to beyond the walls. Just as the schoolroom was decorated with images of Apollo and the Muses, so the palæstra was decorated with images of Hermes, Heracles, and Eros, symbolizing, respectively, adroitness, humane strength, and youthful friendship. The special patron of the palæstra was Hermes, and the gymnastic exhibition took the form of a festival to him, the Hermæa, at which a sacrifice was offered and the boys were allowed the use of the building to play games in, the victors wearing crowns.

It would be impossible, in a work of this compass, to enter into a minute description of all the exercises of the Athenian palæstra. We must be content with a general statement, which may be prefaced with the remark that these exercises were at first light, increasing gradually in rigor and difficulty as the strength and skill of the growing child permitted.

The chief gymnastic exercises were five, named in this order in a famous line of Simonides: (1) leaping, (2) running, (3) discus-throwing, (4) javelin-casting, (5) wrestling ($\pi\acute{a}\lambda\eta$), which last gave the name to the palæstra. We shall not strictly follow this order, but begin with

(1) *Running.*—This was the simplest, lightest, most natural, and, therefore, the most easily taught of exercises. It was probably also the oldest. We find even Homer making his ideal Phæacians begin their games with it, and this practice seems to have been general throughout antiquity. In taking this exercise, the boys divested themselves of all clothing and had their bodies rubbed with oil. The running appears to have been of the simplest kind. Hurdle-races, sack-races, etc., were apparently excluded from education. At the same time, the running was rendered difficult by the soft sand with which the course was covered to the depth of several inches. The races were distinguished according to their length in fur-

longs or stadia: (1) the furlong-race, (2) the double-furlong race, (3) the horse (four-furlong) race, (4) the long race, whose length seems to have been twenty-four furlongs, or about three miles. The stadion was = 202¼ yards English. The shorter races called for brief concentration of energy, the longer for persistence and endurance; all were exercises in agility; all tended to develop lung-power.

(2) *Leaping* or *Jumping.* — This exercise seems, in the main, to have confined itself to the long leap. Though the high leap and the pole-jump can hardly have been unknown, we have no evidence that they were ever employed in the gymnastic training of boys. There may have been hygienic reasons which forbade their use. On the other hand, boys were taught to lengthen their leap by means of weights, somewhat similar to our dumb-bells, carried in their hands, and swung forward in the act of leaping. Such leaping would be an exercise for the arms, as well as for the legs and the rest of the body. But, just as there were two exercises intended chiefly for the legs, so there were two intended chiefly for the arms — discus-throwing and javelin-casting.

(3) *Discus-throwing.* — The modern world has been rendered very familiar with the method of this exercise by the copies of the *discobolus* of Myron, preserved in Rome and extensively engraved and photographed, and that of the *discobolus* of Alcamenes which now stands in the Vatican (see Overbeck, *Griech. Plastik* vol. i, p. 276). The discus was generally a flat, round piece of stone or metal, a sort of large quoit with no hole in the middle, which the user sought to

throw as far as he could. The discobolus of Alcamenes shows us a youth balancing the discus in his
left hand, and taking the measure of his throw with
his eye; that of Myron shows us another in the act of
throwing. He swings the discus backward in his
right hand, and bends his body forward to balance it.
His right foot, the toes contracted with effort, rests
firmly on the ground; the left is slightly lifted; the
whole body is like a bent bow. In the next instant
the left foot will advance, the left hand, now resting
on the right knee, will swing backwards, the body will
resume its erect position, and the discus will be shot
forward from the right hand like an arrow. Nothing
could show more clearly than does this statue the perfect organization, symmetry, and balance which were
the aim of Greek gymnastics. Not one limb could be
moved without affecting all the rest, — which shows
that the exercise extended to the whole body.

(4) *Javelin-casting.* — The aim of this exercise was
to develop skill and precision of eye and hand, rather
than strength of muscle. The instrument employed
was a short dagger or lance, which was aimed at a
mark. He who could hit the mark from the greatest
distance was the most proficient scholar. The spear,
before being thrown, was balanced in the right hand
at the height of the ear.

(5) *Wrestling.* — This very complicated exercise was
evidently the principal one in the gymnastic course,
the one to which the others were merely preparatory.
It was the only one which a boy could not practice
by himself. It exercised not only the whole body,
but the patience and temper as well. The aim of the

wrestler was to throw (καταβάλλειν) his antagonist.
Those who took part in this exercise had their bodies
rubbed with oil and strewn with fine sand. It seems
that the wrestler was allowed to do anything he chose
to his antagonist except to bite, strike, or kick him.
Before he could claim the victory he had to throw him
three times. After the contest the wrestlers scraped
from their bodies, with a strigil, the oil and dust,[1]
bathed, were again rubbed with oil, exposed their
bodies to the sun, in order to dry and tan them, and
dressed. The bathing was done in cold water, and
both the bathing and the sunning were in part intended to inure the body to sudden cold and heat,
which inurement was considered a very essential part
of physical training.

Such were the chief exercises employed in the gymnastic training of the Athenians. Thus far, we have
considered the two branches of education as conducted
separately, and as not coming at any point in contact
with each other. But it would have been very unlike
the Greek, and especially the Athenian, to leave the
two divisions of education unrelated and unharmo-
nized. And, indeed, he did not so leave them, but
brought them together in the most admirable way in
what he called *orchesis*, a word for which we have no
better equivalent than

(γ) *Dancing* (ὄρχησις, χορός).

"Dancers," says Aristotle, "by means of plastic
rhythms (rhythms reproduced in plastic forms) imi-

---

[1] This is represented in the charming Apoxyomenos of the
Vatican.

tate characters, feelings, and actions." Xenophon, in his *Anabasis*, describing a banquet that took place in the wilds of Paphlagonia, says: "After the treaty was ratified and the pæan sung, there first rose up two Thracians and danced in armor to the flute, leaping high and lightly, and using their swords. Finally one of them struck the other, so that everybody thought he had wounded him; but he fell in an artificial way. Then the Paphlagonians raised a shout; but the assailant, having despoiled the fallen man of his armor, went out singing the Sitalcas. Then others of the Thracians carried out the other as if he had been dead; but he was none the worse. Next, some Ænianes and Magnesians stood up and danced the so-called Carpæa in armor. The manner of the dance was this: one man, putting his arms within reach, sows and drives a team, frequently turning round as if afraid. Then a robber makes his appearance. As soon as the other espies him, he seizes his arms, advances to him, and fights in front of the team. And the two did this keeping time to the flute. Finally the robber, having bound the other, carries off both him and the team; sometimes, on the contrary, the ploughman binds the robber, in which case he yokes him, with his hands bound behind his back, to his oxen and drives off." Several other dances, performed by persons of different nationalities, follow; but enough has been quoted to show that the Greek ὄρχησις was something very different from our dancing. It was, indeed, a pantomimic ballet, interspersed with *tableaux vivans*.

In the dances here mentioned, the flute is the instrument employed, and this the player could not

accompany with his voice. But in the Athenian
schools, in the old time, the flute, and all music without words, were tabooed. There can be no doubt,
therefore, that in these the orchestic performances
were accompanied by the lyre, the player on which
sang in words what the dancers danced. It is obvious
that in such performances the musical (literary) and
gymnastic branches of education came in for about
equal shares. Dancing exercised the whole human
being, body and soul, and exercised them in a completely harmonious way. It is this harmony, this
rhythmic movement of the body in consonance with
the emotions of the soul and the purposes of the in-
telligence, that is *grace* ($\chi\acute{\alpha}\rho\iota\varsigma$). Hence, while the
Greeks relied upon gymnastics to impart strength and
firmness to the body, they looked to dancing for court-
liness and grace. Plato places the two on the same
footing, as parts of a single discipline.

The fact that the two divisions of education met
in dancing seems to prove what I surmised above,
viz. that they were conducted within the same precincts; in which case we may suppose that, while the
dancing exercises took place in the palæstra, the music
was supplied by the music master. We know that
the chorus-leader was a public officer, appointed by
the demos, and had to be over forty years old. In any
case, it is curious enough to think that Athenian, and,
generally, Greek, education culminated in dancing.
But this was a perfectly logical result; for the chorus
is the type of Greek social life, as we see most clearly
in the *Republic* of Plato. It hardly needs to be pointed
out that the supreme form of Greek art, the drama,

was but a development of the Bacchic or Dionysiac chorus. This development consisted in the separation of the music from the pantomine, and the assignment of the former to the chorus, which no longer danced, but walked, and of the latter to the actors, who added the dialogue to it. Greek life was divided into three parts — civil, military, religious. Music and letters were a preparation for the first, gymnastics for the second, and dancing for the third. Dancing formed a prominent part in Greek worship, and it may be doubted whether free Athenians ever danced except "before the gods " — ἐν ταῖς πρὸς τοὺς θεοὺς προσόδοις, as Xenophon says.

Two things still remain to be considered with regard to Athenian schools, (1) grading, (2) holidays. With respect to the former, the practice probably differed at different times; but we seem to be justified in assuming that, at the time of which I am speaking, there were but two grades, boys (παῖδες) and youths (νεανίσκοι). These are mentioned by Plato, in the *Lysis*, as celebrating the Hermæa together in a palæstra. The first grade would include the boys from seven to eleven years of age; the second, those from eleven to fifteen. As to holidays, they seem to have been simply the feast-days of the greater gods, when business of every sort was suspended. Such days amounted to about ninety annually.

(3) COLLEGE EDUCATION.

About the time when he was blossoming into manhood, that is, some time between his fourteenth and his sixteenth year, the Athenian boy of the olden time was transferred from the private school and palæstra, which belonged to the family side of life, to the gymnasium, which belonged to the State, and in which he received the education calculated to fit him for the duties of a citizen. Having, in the family and the school, been trained to be a gentleman (καλοκἀγαθός), he must now be trained to be a citizen, capable of exercising legislative, judicial, and military functions. The State saw to it that he received this training, if his parents chose and could afford it.

In the time of Solon, about B.C. 590, two great gymnasia, the Academy and Cynosarges, were erected in the midst of extensive groves outside the city walls. These groves were afterwards surrounded with high walls, furnished with seats and other conveniences, and turned into city parks. The Academy, which lay to the northwest of the city, in the valley of the Cephisus, and was under the patronage of Athena, was the resort of the full-blooded citizens, while Cynosarges, situated to the east of the city, near the foot of Lycabettus, was assigned to those who had foreign blood in their veins, that is, who had only one parent of pure Athenian stock. This gymnasium was under the patronage of Heracles, whose worship always implies the presence of a foreign and vanquished element. These were the only two gymnasia belonging to Athens before the time of Pericles. They were, probably, destroyed by the Persians in 480, and had afterwards to be rebuilt, and the groves replanted.

While the children of nearly all the free citizens of Athens attended the school and the palæstra, it is clear that only the youth of the wealthier classes attended the gymnasium. One result of this was that the government and offices of the State fell exclusively into the hands of those classes; and it was perhaps just in order to make this division, without introducing any class-law, that the shrewd Solon established the gymnasia, which thus became a bulwark against democracy.

As soon as the Athenian youth was transferred to the gymnasium, he passed from under the charge of the pedagogue, who represented the family, and came under the direct surveillance of the State. He was now free to go where he would, to frequent the agora and the street, to attend the theatre, in which he had his appointed place, and to make himself directly acquainted with all the details of public life. In the gymnasium he passed into the hands of a gymnast or scientific trainer, and for the next two or three years was subjected to the severer exercises, wrestling, boxing, etc. No special provision, beyond the fact that he had to learn the laws, was made for his intellectual and moral instruction. He was expected to acquire this from contact with the older citizens whom he met in the agora, the street, or the public park. Thus, at what is justly regarded as the most critical age, he was almost compelled to live a free, breezy, outdoor life, full of activity and stirring incident, his thoughts and feelings directed outwards into acts of will, and not turned back upon himself or his own states. At the same time he was acquiring just that practical knowledge of ethical laws and of real life which could best fit him for active citizenship. He now learnt to ride, to drive, to row, to swim, to attend banquets, to sustain a conversation, to discuss the weightiest questions of statesmanship, to sing and dance in public choruses, and to ride or walk in public processions. If he abused his liberty and behaved in a lawless or unseemly way, he was called to account by the severe Court of the Areopagus, which attended to public morals. He saw little of girls of his own age, except his sisters, unless it was at public festivals, when there was little opportunity of becoming acquainted with them. His affectionate nature therefore expressed itself mostly in the form of devoted friendships to other youths of his own, or nearly his own, age, a fact which enables us to understand why friendship fills so large a space, not only in the life, but also in the ethical treatises of the Greeks, — Plato, Aristotle, etc., — and why love, in the modern sense, plays so insignificant a part. The truth is that, even in Athens, the State encroached upon the family. Plato's *Republic* was only the logical carrying out of principles that were latent long before in the social life of the Athenian people.

It would be impossible to treat in detail the exercises to which the Athenian youth was subjected during the years in which he attended the public gymnasium as a pupil. The old exercises of the palæstra were continued, running and wrestling especially; but the former was now done in armor, and the latter became more violent, and was supplemented by boxing. In fact, the physical exercises were now systematized into the *pentathlon* — running, leaping, discus-throwing, wrestling, boxing — which formed

the programme of nearly all gymnastic exhibitions.
During these years, the youth was still regarded as a
minor, and his father or guardian was responsible for
his good behavior.   But when he reached the age of
eighteen, a change took place, and he passed under
the direct control of the State.   His father now
brought him before the reeve of his *demos* (ward or
village), as a candidate for independent citizenship.
If he proved to be the lawful child of free citizens,
and came up to the moral and physical requirements
of the law, his name was entered upon the register of
the demos, and he became a member of it.   He was
now prepared to be presented to the whole people, and
to pass the State examination.   He shore his long
hair for the first time, and donned the black garment
of the citizen.   In this guise he presented himself to
the king-archon of the State, who, at a public assembly, introduced him, along with others, to the whole
people.   He was then and there armed with spear
and shield (supplied by the State if his father had
fallen in war), and thence proceeded to the shrine of
Aglauros, where, looking down on the agora, the city,
and the Attic plain, he took the Solonian oath of
citizenship (see p. 61).   He was now technically
an *ephēbos*, cadet, or citizen-novice, ready to undergo
those two years of severe discipline which at once
formed his introduction to practical affairs, and con-
stituted the State examination.   During the first year
he remained in the neighborhood of Athens, drilling
in arms, and acquiring a knowledge of military
tactics.   His life was now the hard life of a soldier.
He slept in the open air, or in the guard-houses

(φρούρια) that surrounded the city, and was liable to
be called upon at any time by the government to give
aid in an emergency. He also took part in the public
festivals. At the end of the year, all the *ephēboi* of
one year's standing passed an examination in military drill before the assembled people (ἀπεδείξαντο τῷ
δήμῳ περὶ τὰς τάξεις [1]), after which they were employed
as militia to man the frontier guard-houses, and as
rural *gendarmerie* (περίπολοι), scouring the country in
all directions. They now lived like soldiers in war-
time, and learnt two important things, (1) the topog-
raphy of Attica, its roads, passes, brooks, springs,
etc., (2) the art of enforcing law and order. Their
life, indeed, closely resembled that of the Alpine
corps (*Alpini*) of the Italian army at the present day.
These spend the summer in making themselves acquainted with every height, valley, pass, stream, and
covert in the Italian Alps, often bivouacking for days
together at great heights. That during this time the
ephēboi should have taken any part in the legislative
or judicial duties of citizens, seems in the highest
degree improbable. At the end of their second year,
however, they passed a second examination, called the
citizenship or manhood examination (δοκιμασία εἰς
ἄνδρας), after which they were full members of the
State.

(4) University Education.

The Greek university was the State, and the Greek
State was a university — a *Cultur-Staat*, as the Ger-

---

[1] So says Aristotle, who tells us further that in his time on this
occasion they were presented with spear and shield *by the people*
(see p. 97).

mans say. That the State is a school of virtue, was a view generally entertained in the ancient world, which, until it began to decay, completely identified the man with the citizen. The influence of this view upon the attitude of the individual to the State, and of the State to the individual, can hardly be over-estimated. The State claimed, and the individual accorded to it, a disciplinary right which extended to every sphere and action of life. Thus the sphere of morality coincided exactly with the sphere of legality, or, to put it the other way, the sphere of legality extended to the whole sphere of morality, and this was considered true, whatever form the State or government might assume — monarchy, aristocracy, democracy, etc.

To give a full account of the university education of old Athens would be to write her social and political history up to the time of the Persian Wars. This is, of course, out of the question. All I can do is to point out those elements in the State which enabled it to produce that splendid array of noble men, and accomplish those great deeds and works, which make her brief career seem the brightest spot in the world's history.

The chief of these elements, and the one which included all the rest, was the Greek ideal of harmony. Athens was great as a State and as a school so long as she embodied that ideal, so long as she distributed power and honor in accordance with worth (ἀρετή) intellectual, moral, practical; in a word, so long as the State was governed by the best citizens (ἄριστοι), and the rest acknowledged their right to do so. Notwithstanding the contention of Grote and others, it is strictly true that Athens was great because, and so long as, she was aristocratic (in the ancient sense), and perished when she abandoned her fundamental ideal by becoming democratic. This assertion must not be construed as any slur upon democracy as such, or as denying that Athens in perishing paved the way for a higher ideal than her own. It simply states a fact, which may be easily generalized without losing its truth: An institution perishes when it abandons the principle on which it was founded and built up. Unless we bear this in mind, we shall utterly fail to understand the lesson of Athenian history. If it be maintained that some of Athens' noblest work was done under the democracy, the sufficient answer is, that it was nearly all done by men who retained the spirit of the old aristocracy, and bitterly opposed the democracy. We need name only Æschylus, Sophocles, Aristophanes, Plato, Aristotle, Demosthenes.

PART II

THE "NEW EDUCATION" (B.C. 480–338)

CHAPTER I

INDIVIDUALISM AND PHILOSOPHY

Homer ought to be driven from the lists and whipt, and Archilochus likewise. — HERACLITUS.

> Thou needs must have knowledge of all things,
> First of the steadfast core of the Truth that forceth conviction,
> Then of the notions of mortals, where true conviction abides not.
> — PARMENIDES.

All things were undistinguished : then Intellect came and brought them into order. — ANAXAGORAS.

Man is the measure of all things.

In regard to the Gods, I am unable to know whether they are or are not. — PROTAGORAS.

STREPSIADES. Don't you see what a good thing it is to have learning? There isn't any Zeus, Phidippides !

PHIDIPPIDES. Who is there then?

STREPS. Vortex rules, having dethroned Zeus.

PHID. Pshaw! what nonsense!

STREPS. You may count it true, all the same.

PHID. Who says so?

STREPS. Socrates the Melian, and Chærephon, who knows the footprints of fleas. — ARISTOPHANES, *Clouds*.

There is an old-fashioned saw, current of yore among mortals, that a man's happiness, when full-grown, gives birth and dies not childless, and that from Fortune there springs insatiate woe for all his race. But I, dissenting from all others, am alone of differ-

ent mind. It is the Irreverent Deed that begets after it more of its
kind. For to righteous homes belongs a fair-childrened lot forever;
but old Irreverence is sure to beget Irreverence, springing up fresh
among evil men, when the numbered hour arrives. And the new
Irreverence begets Surfeit of Wealth, and a power beyond all battle,
beyond all war, unholy Daring, twin curses, black to homes, like
to their parents. But Justice shines in smoky homes, and honors
the righteous life, and, leaving, with averted eyes, foundations
gilded with impurity of hands, she draws nigh to holy things,
honoring not the power of wealth, with its counterfeit stamp of
praise. And her will is done. — Æschylus.

From the time they are children to the day of their death,
we teach them and admonish them. As soon as the child under-
stands what is said to him, his nurse and his mother and his pedagogue and even his father vie with each other in trying to make the
best of him that can be made, at every word and deed instructing
him and warning him, "This is right," "This is wrong," "This is
beautiful," "This is ugly," "This is righteous," "This is sinful,"
"Do this," "Don't do that." And if the child readily obeys, well
and good; if he does not, then they treat him like a bent and twisted
stick, straightening him out with threats and blows. Later on, they
send him to school, and then they lay their injunctions upon the
masters to pay much more attention to the good behavior of their
sons than to their letters and music (κιθάρισις); and the teachers act
upon these injunctions. Later yet, when they have learnt to read,
and are proceeding to understand the meaning of what is written,
just as formerly they understood what was said to them, they put
before them on the benches to read the works of good poets, and
insist upon their learning them by heart — works which contain
many admonitions, and many narratives, noble deeds, and eulogies
of the worthy men of old — their purpose being to awaken the boy's
ambition, so that he may imitate these men and strive to be worthy
likewise. The music-teachers also, pursuing the same line, try to
inculcate self-control (σωφροσύνη) and to prevent the boys from falling into mischief. In addition to this, when they have learnt to
play on the lyre, their masters teach them other poems, written by
great lyric poets, making them sing them and play the accompani-
ments to them, and compelling them to work into their souls the
rhythms and melodies of them, so that they may grow in gentleness, and, having their natures timed and tuned, may be fitted to
speak and act. The truth is, the whole life of man needs timing

and tuning. Furthermore, in addition to all this, parents send their sons to the physical trainer, in order that their bodies may be improved and rendered capable of seconding a noble intent, and they themselves not be forced, from physical deterioration, to play the coward in war or other (serious) matters. And those who can best afford to give this education, give most of it, and these are the richest people. Their sons go earliest to school and leave it latest. And when the boys leave school, the State insists that they shall learn the laws and live according to them, and not according to their own caprice. . . . And if any one transgresses these laws, the State punishes him. . . . Seeing that so much attention is devoted to virtue, both in the family and in the State, do you wonder, Socrates, and question whether virtue be something that can be taught? Surely you ought not to wonder at this, but rather to wonder if it could *not* be taught.—PLATO, *Protagoras* (*words of Protagoras*).

"Isn't it true, Lysis," said I, "that your parents love you very much?"—"To be sure," said he.—"Then they would wish you to be as happy as possible?"—"Of course," said he.—"And do you think a person is happy who is a slave, and is not allowed to do anything he desires?"—"I don't, indeed," said he.—"Then, if your father and mother love you and wish you to be happy, they endeavor by every means in their power to make you happy."—"To be sure they do," said he.—"Then they allow you to do anything you please, and never chide you, or prevent you from doing what you desire."—"By Jove! they do, Socrates: they prevent me from doing a great many things."—"What do you mean," said I; "they wish you to be happy, and yet prevent you from doing what you wish? Let us take an example: If you want to ride in one of your father's chariots, and to hold the reins, when it is competing in a race, won't they allow you, or will they prevent you?"—"By Jove! no: they would not allow me," said he. "But why should they? There is a charioteer, who is hired by my father."—"What do you mean? They allow a hired man, rather than you, to do what he likes with the horses, and pay him a salary besides?"—"And why not?" said he.—"Well then, I suppose they allow you to manage the mule-team, and if you wanted to take the whip and whip it, they would permit you."—"How could they?" said he.—"What?" said I: "is nobody allowed to whip it?"—"Of course," he said; "the muleteer."—"A slave or a free man?"—"A slave," said he.—"And so it seems they think more of a slave than of their son, and entrust their property to him rather than to you, and allow him to do what he pleases, whereas they prevent you. But, farther, tell me this. Do they allow you to manage yourself, or do they not even trust you to that extent?" — "How trust me?" said he. — "Then does some one manage you?" — "Yes, my pedagogue here," said he. — "But he is surely not a slave?" — "Of course he is, our slave," said he. — "Is it not strange," said I, "that a free-man should be governed by a slave? But, to continue, what is this pedagogue doing when he governs you?" — "Taking me to a teacher, or something of the kind," he said. — "And these teachers, it cannot be that they too govern you?" — "To any extent." — "So then your father likes to set over you a host of masters and managers; but, of course, when you go home to your mother, she lets you do what you like, in order to make you happy, either with the threads or the loom, when she is weaving — does she not? She surely doesn't in the least prevent you from handling the batten, or the comb, or any of the instruments used in spinning." — And he, laughing, said: "By Jove, Socrates; she not only prevents me, but I should be beaten if I touched them." — "By Hercules," said I, "isn't it true that you have done some wrong to your father and mother?" — "By Jove, not I," he said. — "But for what reason, then, do they so anxiously prevent you from being happy, and doing what you please, and maintain you the whole day in servi-tude to some one or another, and without power to do almost any-thing you like. It seems, indeed, that you derive no advantage from all this wealth, but anybody manages it rather than you, nor from your body, nobly born as it is, but some one else shepherds it and takes care of it. But you govern nothing, Lysis, and do noth-ing that you desire." — "The reason, Socrates," he said, "is, that I am not of age." — PLATO, *Lysis.*

The present state of the constitution is as follows: Citizenship is a right of children whose parents are both of them citizens. Regis-tration as member of a deme or township takes place when eigh-teen years of age are completed. Before it takes place the towns-men of the deme find a verdict on oath, firstly, whether they believe the youth to be as old as the law requires, and if the ver-dict is in the negative he returns to the ranks of the boys. Secondly, the jury find whether he is freeborn and legitimate. If the verdict is against him he appeals to the Heliæa, and the muni-cipality delegate five of their body to accuse him of illegitimacy. If he is found by the jurors to have been illegally proposed for the register, the State sells him for a slave; if the judgment is given in his favor, he must be registered as one of the municipality. Those on the register are afterwards examined by the senate, and if any-one is found not to be eighteen years old, a fine is imposed on the municipality by which he was registered. After approbation, they are called *epheboi*, or cadets, and the parents of all who belong to a single tribe hold a meeting and, after being sworn, choose three men of the tribe above forty years of age, whom they believe to be of stainless character and fittest for the superintendence of youth, and out of these the commons in ecclesia select one superin-tendent for all of each tribe, and a governor of the whole body of youths from the general body of the Athenians. These take them in charge, and after visiting with them all the temples, march down to Piræus, where they garrison the north and south harbors, Munychia and Acte. The commons also elect two gymnastic trainers for them, and persons who teach them to fight in heavy armor, to draw the bow, to throw the javelin, and to handle artil-lery. Each of the ten commanders receives as pay a drachma [about 20 cts.] per diem, and each of the cadets four obols [about 13 cts.]. Each commander draws the pay of the cadets of his own tribe, buys with it the necessaries of life for the whole band (for they mess together by tribes), and purveys for all their wants. The first year is spent in military exercises. The second year the com-mons meet in the theatre and the cadets, after displaying before them their mastery in warlike evolutions, are each presented with a shield and spear, and become mounted patrols of the frontier and garrison the fortresses. They perform this service for two years, wearing the equestrian cloak and enjoying immunity from civic functions. During this period, to guard their military duties from interruption, they can be parties to no action either as defendant or plaintiff, except in suits respecting inheritance, or heiresses, or suc-cessions to hereditary priesthoods. When the three years are com-pleted they fall into the ordinary body of citizens. — ARISTOTLE, *Constitution of Athens (Poste's Version, with slight alterations)*.

THAT perfect harmony between power and worth at which the Athenian State aimed, was something not easily attained or preserved. As far back as its recorded history reaches, we find a struggle for

power going on between a party which possessed
more power than its worth justified, and a party which
possessed less; that is, between a party which, having
once been worthy, strove to hold power in virtue of
its past history, and one that claimed power in virtue
of the worth into which it was growing: in a word, a
struggle between declining aristocracy and growing
democracy. To the party in power, of course, this
seemed a rebellion against lawful authority and privilege, and it did its best to suppress it. Hence came
the rigorous legislation of Draco; later the more con-
ciliatory, less out-spoken, but equally aristocratic
legislation of Solon; then the tyranny of Pisistratus,
lasting as long as he could hold the balance of power
between the contending parties; then the constitution
of Clisthenes, with the breaking up of the old Athenian aristocratic system, the remodelling of the tribes,
the degradation of the Areopagus, and the definite
triumph of democracy. To complete the movement
and, as it were, to consecrate it, came the Persian
Wars, which mark the turning-point, the *peripeteia*,
in Athenian history and education. Whatever efforts
aristocracy makes to maintain itself after this, are
made in the name of, and under cover of a zeal for,
democracy.

The aristocratic Athenian State was based upon
land-ownership, slavery, and the entire freedom of
the land-owning class from all but family and State
duties, from all need of engaging in productive industry. So long as the chief wealth of the State consisted
in land and its produce, so long the population was
divided into two classes, the rich and the poor, and

so long the former had little difficulty in keeping all power in its own hands. But no sooner did the growth of commerce throw wealth into the hands of a class that owned no land, and was not above engaging in industry, than this class began to claim a share in political power. There were now two wealthy classes, standing opposed to each other, a proud, conservative one, with "old wealth and worth," and a vain, radical one, with new wealth and wants, both bidding for the favor of the class that had little wealth, little worth, and many wants, and thus making it feel its importance. Such is the origin of Athenian democracy. It is the child of trade and productive industry. It owed its final consecration to the Persian Wars, and especially to the battle of Salamis, in which Athens was saved by her fleet, manned chiefly by marines (ἐπιβάται) from the lower classes, the upper classes, as we have seen, being trained only for land-service. Thus the battle of Salamis was not only a victory of Greece over Persia, but of foreign trade over home agriculture, of democracy over aristocracy.

The fact that the Athenian democracy owed its origin to trade determined, in great measure, its history and tendencies. One of its many results was that it opened Athens to the influx of foreign men, foreign ideas, and foreign habits, not to speak of foreign gods, all of which tended to break up the old self-contained, carefully organized life of the people. In no department were their effects sooner or more clearly felt than in that of education. From about the date of the battle of Salamis, when the youthful Ionian, Anaxagoras, came to Athens, a succession of

men of "advanced" ideas in art and science sought a
field of action within her borders. Such a field, indeed, seemed purposely to have been left open for
them by the State, which had provided no means of
intellectual or moral education for its young citizens,
after they passed under its care (see p. 87). Nothing
was easier or more profitable than for these wise foreigners to constitute themselves public teachers, and
fill the place which the State had left vacant. The
State might occasionally object, and seek to punish
one or another of them for corrupting of the youth by
the promulgation of impious or otherwise dangerous
ideas, as it did in the case of Anaxagoras; but their
activity was too much in harmony with a tendency of
the time, — a radical and individualistic tendency
inseparable from democracy, — to be dispensed with
altogether. Hence it was that, within a few years
after the battle of Salamis, there flourished in Athens
a class of men unknown before within her boundaries,
a class of private professors, or "sophists," as they
called themselves, who undertook to teach theoretically
what the State had assumed could be taught only practically and by herself, viz., virtue and wisdom. Their
ideas were novel, striking, and radical, hence conge-
nial to a newly emancipated populace, vain of its recent
achievements, and contemptuous of all that savored of
the narrow, pious puritanism of the old time; their
premises were magnificent, and their fees high enough
to impose upon a class that always measures the
value of a thing by what it is asked to pay for it;
their method of teaching was such as to flatter the
vanity, and secure the favor, of both pupils and

parents. No wonder that their success was immediate and their influence enormous.

From the days of Socrates to our own, 'sophist' has been a term of reproach, and not altogether unjustly so. Hegel, Grote, and Zeller have, indeed, shown that the sophists did not deserve all the obloquy which has attached itself to their name, inasmuch as they were neither much better nor much worse than any class of men who set up to teach new doctrines for money, and, as wise economists, suit supply to demand; nevertheless, it may be fairly enough said that they largely contributed to demoralize Athens, by encouraging irreverence for the very conceptions upon which her polity was built, and by pandering to some of the most selfish and individualistic tendencies of democracy. If it be said that they have their place in the history of human evolution, as the heralds of that higher view of life which allows the individual a sphere of activities and interests outside of that occupied by the State, this may at once and without difficulty be admitted, without our being thereby forced to regard them as noble men. The truth is, they represented, in practice and in theory, the spirit of individualism, which was then everywhere asserting itself against the spirit of nationalism or polity, and which perhaps had to assert itself in an exaggerated and destructive way, before the rightful claims of the two could be manifested and harmonized. It is the incorporation of this spirit of individualism into education that constitutes the "New Education."

This spirit, as manifested in the sophists and their teaching, directed itself against the old political spirit

KANSAS CITY UNIVERSITY LIBRARY

in all the departments of life—in religion, in politics,
in education. It discredited the old popular gods,
upon loyalty to whom the existence of the State had
been supposed to depend, substituting for them some
crude fancy like Vortex, or some bald abstraction like
Intellect. It encouraged the individual to seek his
end in his own pleasure, and to regard the State as
but a means to that end. It championed an education in which these ideas occupied a prominent place.
What the sophists actually taught the ambitious young
men who sought their instruction, was self-assertion,
unscrupulousness, and a showy rhetoric, in whose
triumphal procession facts, fancies, and falsehoods
marched together in brilliant array. It is but fair to
them to say that, in their endeavor to instruct young
men in the art of specious oratory, they laid the foundations of the art of rhetoric and the science of grammar. So much, at least, the world owes to them.

Since it was to the young men, who, freed from the
discipline of home, pedagogue, school, and palæstra,
could be met with anywhere, in the street, the agora,
the gymnasium, that the sophists directed their chief
attention, it was of course these who first showed the
effects of their teaching. But their influence, falling
in, as it did, with the pronounced radical tendencies
of the time, soon made itself felt in all grades of education, from the family to the university, in the form
of an irreverent, flippant, conceited rationalism, before
whose self-erected and self-corrupted tribunal every
institution in heaven and earth was to be tried. In
the schools this influence showed itself in various
ways: (1) in an increased attention to literature, and

especially to the formal side of it, (2) in the tendency to substitute for the works of the old epic and lyric poets the works of more recent writers tinged with the new spirit, (3) in the introduction of new and complicated instruments and kinds of music, (4) in an increasing departure from the severe physical and moral discipline of the old days. We now, for the first time, hear of a teacher of literature, distinct from the music master, of teachers who possessed no copy of Homer (Alcibiades is said to have chastised such a one), of flutes, citharas, and the like in use in schools, of wildness and lewdness among boys of tender age. In the palæstra the new spirit showed itself in a tendency to substitute showy and unsystematic exercises for the vigorous and graded exercises of the older time, to sacrifice education to execution.

But, as already remarked, the new spirit showed itself most clearly and hurtfully in the higher education. The young men, instead of spending their time in vigorous physical exercise in the gymnasia and open country, began now to hang about the streets and public places, listening to sophistic discussions, and to attend the schools of the sophists, exercising their tongues more than any other part of their bodies. The effect of this soon showed itself in a decline of physical power, of endurance, courage, and manliness, and in a strong tendency to luxury and other physical sins. They now began to imagine for themselves a private life, very far from coincident with that demanded of a citizen, and to look upon the old citizen-life, and its ideals, sanctions, and duties, with contempt or pity, as something which they had learnt to rise above.

The glory and well-being of their country were no longer their chief object of ambition. The dry rot of individualism, which always seems to those affected by it an evidence of health and manly vigor, was corrupting their moral nature, and preparing the way for the destruction of the State. For it was but too natural that these young men, when they came to be members of the State, should neglect its lessons and claims, and, following the new teachings, live to themselves. Thus, just as the character of the "Old Education" of Athens showed itself in the behavior of her sons in the Persian Wars, so that of her "New Education" showed itself fifty years later in the Peloponnesian War, that long and disastrous struggle which wrecked Athens and Greece.

Yet Athens and her education were not allowed to go to ruin without a struggle. The aristocratic party long stuck to the old principles and tried to give them effect; but, failing to understand the new circumstances and to take account of them, it erred in the application of them, by seeking simply to restore the old conditions. Individuals also exerted their best efforts for the same end. Æschylus, who had fought at Marathon, and who, more than any other Greek, was endowed with the spirit of religion, interpreted the old mythology in an ethical sense, and in this form worked it into a series of dramas, whereby the history and institutions of the Greek people were shown to be due to a guiding Providence of inexorable justice, rewarding each man according to his works, abhorring proud homes "gilded with impurity of hands," and dwelling with the pure and righteous, though housed in the meanest cot. Æschylus thus became, not only the father of Greek tragedy, but also the sublimest moral teacher Greece ever possessed. For moral grandeur there is but one work in all literature that can stand by the side of Æschylus' *Oresteia*, and that is the *Divine Comedy*. Yet Æschylus was driven from Athens on a charge of impiety, and died in exile.

But it was not the tragic drama alone that was inspired and made a preacher of righteousness: in the hands of Aristophanes, the comic drama exerted all its power for the same end. For over thirty years this inimitable humorist used the public theatre to lash the follies, and hold up to contempt the wretched leaders, of the Athenian populace, pointing out to his countrymen the abyss of destruction that was yawning before them. The world has never seen such earnest comedy, not even in the works of Molière or Beaumarchais. Yet it was all in vain. Long before his death, Aristophanes was forbidden to hold up to public scorn the degradation of his people.

Among the individual citizens who labored with all their might to bring back Athens to her old worth were two of very different character, endowments, and position, the one laboring in the world of action, the other in the world of thought. The first was Pericles, who, seeing that democracy was the order of the day, accepted it, and, by his personal character and position, strove to guide it to worthy ends. In order to encourage gymnastic exercises, particularly among the sons of the newer families, he built the Lyceum, in a grove sacred to Apollo, between Cynosarges and the city walls, as a gymnasium for them.

With a view to encouraging among them the study of music, he built an odeon, or music-hall, under the southeast end of the Acropolis. Both were magnificent structures. What he did towards the completion of the great theatre for the encouragement of dancing, we do not know; that this entered into his plan, there can hardly be any doubt. But Pericles was too wise a man to suppose that he could induce his pleasure-seeking countrymen to subject themselves to the old discipline, without offering them an object calculated to rouse their ambition and call forth their energy. This object was nothing less than a united Greece, with Athens as its capital. How hard he tried to make this object familiar to them, and to render Athens worthy of the place he desired her to occupy, is pathetically attested to this day by the Propylæa and the Parthenon. On the frieze of the latter is represented the solemn sacrifice that was to cement the union of the Hellenic people, and place it at the head of civilization. When degenerate Greece resisted all his efforts to make her become one peaceably, he tried to make her do so by force, and the Peloponnesian War, started on a mere frivolous pretext, was the result. He did not live long enough to learn the outcome of this desperate attempt to wake his countrymen to new moral and political life, and it was well. If he had, he might have been forced to recognize that he had been attempting an impossible task, — trying to erect a strong structure with rotten timber, to make a noble State out of ignoble, selfish men. Unfortunately, the example of his own private life, in which he openly defied one of the laws of the

State, and tried to make concubinage (ἑταίρησις) respectable, more than undid all the good he sought to accomplish. The truth is, Pericles was himself too deeply imbued with the three vices of his time — rationalism, self-indulgence, and love of show — to be able to see any true remedy for the evils that sprang from them. What was needed was not letters, music, gymnastics, dancing, or dream of empire, but something entirely different — a new moral inspiration and ideal.

This, the second of the men to whom reference has been made, Socrates, sought to supply. In the midst of self-indulgence, he lived a life of poverty and privation; in the midst of splendor and the worship of outward beauty, he pursued simplicity and took pleasure in his ugliness; in the midst of self-assertive rationalism and all-knowing sophistry, he professed ignorance and submission to the gods. The problem of how to restore the moral life of Athens and Greece presented itself to Socrates in this form: *The old ethical social sanctions, divine and human, having, under the influence of rationalism and individualism, lost their power, where and how shall we find other sanctions to take their place?* To answer this one question was the aim of Socrates' whole life. He was not long in seeing that any true answer must rest upon a comprehension of man's entire nature and relations, and that the sophists were able to impose upon his countrymen only because no such comprehension was theirs. He saw that the old moral life, based upon naïve tradition and prescription, sanctioned by gods of the imagination, would have to give place to a moral life resting upon self-understanding and reflection. He accordingly adopted as his motto the command of the Delphic oracle, *Know Thyself* (γνῶθι σεαυτόν), and set to work with all his might to obey it.

He now, therefore, went to meet the sophists on their own ground and with their own methods, and he did this so well as to be considered by many, Aristophanes among them, as the best possible representative of the class. What is true is, that he was the first Athenian who undertook to do what the sophists had for some time considered their special function, — to impart a "higher education" to the youth and men of Athens. He went about the streets, shops, walks, schools, and gymnasia of the city, drawing all sorts of persons into conversation, and trying to elicit truth for himself and them (for he pretended to know nothing). He was never so pleased as when he met a real sophist, who professed to have knowledge, and never so much in his element as when, in the presence of a knot of young men, he could, by his ironical, subtle questions, force said sophist to admit that he too knew nothing. The fact was, Socrates, studying Heraclitus, had become convinced that the reason why men fell into error was because they did not know themselves, or their own thoughts, because what they called thoughts were mere opinions, mere fragments of thoughts. He concluded that, if men were ever to be redeemed from error, intellectual and moral, they must be made to think whole thoughts. Accordingly, he took the ordinary opinions of men and, by a series of well-directed questions, tried to bring out their implications, that is, the wholes of which they were parts. Such is the Socratic or dialectic (= conversational) method. It does not pretend to impart any new knowledge, but merely, as Socrates said, to deliver the mind of the thoughts with which it is pregnant. And Socrates not only held that saving truth consisted of whole thoughts; he held also that all such thoughts were universally and necessarily true; that, while there might be many opinions about a thing, there could be but one truth, the same for all men, and therefore independent of any man. This was the exact opposite of what Protagoras the sophist had taught, the opposite of the gospel of individualism (see p. 93). Man is so far from being the measure of all things, that there is in all things a measure to which he must conform, if he is not to sink into error. This measure, this system of whole truths, implying an eternal mind to which it is present, and by which it is manifested in the world, is just what man arrives at, if he will but think out his thoughts in their completeness. In doing so, he at once learns the laws by which the universe is governed and finds a guide and sanction for his own conduct — a sanction no longer external and imposed by the State, but internal and imposed by the mind. A system like this involved a complete reversal of the old view of the relation between man and the State, and at the same time took the feet from under individualism. "It is true," said Socrates in effect, "that the individual, and not the State, is the source of all authority, the measure of all things; but he is so, not as individual, but as endowed with the universal reason by which the world, including the State, is gov-

erned." This is the sum and substance of Socrates'
teaching, this is what he believed to be true self-
knowledge. This is the truth whose application to
life begins a new epoch in human history, and sepa-
rates the modern from the ancient world; this is the
truth that, reiterated and vivified by Christianity,
forms the very life of our life to-day.

In adopting this view, Socrates necessarily formed
"a party by himself," a party which could hope for
no sympathy from either of the other two into which
his countrymen were divided. The party of tradition
charged him with denying the gods of his country and
corrupting her youth; the radical party hated him
because he convicted its champions of vanity, super-
ficiality, and ignorance. Between them, they com-
passed his death, and Athens learnt, only when it was
too late, that she had slain her prophet. But Socrates,
though slain, was not dead. His spirit lived on, and
the work which he had begun grew and prospered.
Yet it could not save Athens, except upon a condition
which she neither would nor could accept, that of
remodelling her polity and the life of her citizens in
accordance with divine truth and justice. Indeed,
though he discovered a great truth, Socrates did not
present it in a form in which it could be accepted
under the given conditions. He himself even did not
by any means see all the stupendous implications of
his own principle, which, in fact, was nothing less than
the ground of all true ethics, all liberty, and all science. It is doubtful whether any one sees them now,
and certain that they have been nowhere realized.
Still his truth and his life were not without their im-

mediate effect upon Athens and Athenian education. Men, working in his spirit, and inspired with his truth, more or less clearly understood, almost immediately replaced the sophists in Athens, and drew the attention of her citizens, old and young, to the serious search for truth. In fact, from this time on, the intellectual tendency began to prevail over the gymnastic and musical, and this continued until, finally, it absorbed the whole life of the people, and Athens, from being a university-State, became a State-university. Such it was in the days of Cicero, Paul, Plutarch, Lucian, and Proclus. That this one-sided tendency was fatal to the political life of Athens, and therefore, in some degree, to its moral life, is clear enough; and, though we cannot hold Socrates personally responsible for this result, we must still admit that it was one which flowed from his system of thought. Personally, indeed, Socrates was a moral hero, and "five righteous" men like him, had they appeared, would have gone far to save Athens; but this very heroism, this inborn enthusiasm for righteousness, blinded him so far as to make him believe that men had only to know the right in order to be ready to follow it. Hence that exaggerated importance attached to right knowing, and that comparative neglect of right feeling and right doing, which in the sequel proved so paralyzing. Hence the failure of Socrates' teaching to stem the tide of corruption in Athens, and restore her people to heroism and worth.

Socrates left behind him many disciples, some of whom distinguished themselves in practical ways, others as founders of philosophic schools, emphasizing different sides of his teaching. He was but a few years in his grave when two of these were teaching regularly in the two old gymnasia of Athens. Plato, a full-blooded Athenian, was teaching in the Academy the intellectual and moral theories of his master, while Antisthenes, a half-breed (his mother being a Thracian), was inculcating the lesson of his heroic life in Cynosarges. Their followers were called, respectively, Academics and Cynics. Thus, by these two men, was the higher education for the first time introduced into the public institutions of Athens.

Socrates' aim, as we have seen, had been purely a moral one, and this fact was not lost sight of by his immediate followers. The chief question with them all was still: How can the people be brought back to moral life? But, thanks partly to the vagueness in which he had left the details of his doctrine, they were divided with respect to the means whereby this was to be accomplished. One party, best represented by Plato, and following most closely in the footsteps of the master, held that, man being essentially a social being, and morality a relation in society, it was only in and through a social order, a State, that virtue could be realized. Another party, represented by Antisthenes, maintained that virtue was a purely personal matter, and that the wise man stood high above any and all social institutions. These two views maintained themselves, side by side, in nearly all subsequent Greek thought, and at last found expression in the State and Church of the Christian world.

Two of Socrates' followers, believers in institutional morality, left behind them treatises which have come down to us, giving their views as to the manner in which virtue might be cultivated. These are the practical Xenophon and the theoretic Plato, both men of pure Athenian stock. Nothing will better enable us to comprehend the evils of the "New Education" than a consideration of the means by which these worthy men proposed to remedy them. Both are idealists and Utopians; but the former is conservative and reactionary, while the latter is speculative and progressive. Both are aiming at one thing — a virtuous and happy State, to replace the vicious and wretched one in which they found their lot cast; but they differ in their views regarding the nature of such a State, and the means of realizing it.

CHAPTER II

XENOPHON

Never a good is the rule of the many; let one be the ruler. — HOMER.

Wealth without Worth is no harmless housemate. — SAPPHO.

One to me is ten thousand, if he be best.

All the Ephesians, from youth up, ought to be hanged and the State left to the boys, because they cast out Hermodorus, the worthiest man amongst them, saying: ‘No one of us shall be worthiest, else let him be so elsewhere and among others.’ — HERACLITUS.

Reflecting once that, of the very small states, Sparta appeared to be the most powerful and the most renowned in Greece, I began to wonder in what way this had come about. But when I reflected upon the manners of the Spartans, I ceased to wonder. As to Lycurgus, who drew up for them the laws, by obedience to which they have prospered, I admire him and hold him to be, in the highest degree, a wise man. For he, instead of imitating other states, reached conclusions opposite to those of most, and thereby rendered his country conspicuous for prosperity. — XENOPHON.

XENOPHON was in no sense a philosopher or a practical teacher, but he was a man of sterling worth, of knightly courage, of wide and varied experience, of strong sagacity, and of genial disposition, a keen observer, and a charming writer. He was a true old Athenian puritan, broadened and softened by study and contact with the world. He hated democracy so cordially that he would not live in Athens to witness its vulgarity and disorder; but he loved his coun-

114

try, and desired to see its people restored to their ancient worth. He believed that this could be done only by some great, royal personality, like Lycurgus or Cyrus, enforcing a rigid discipline, and once more reducing the man to the citizen. Unwilling, probably, to hold up hated Sparta as a model to his beaten and smarting countrymen, he laid the scene of his pedagogical romance in far-off Persia.

In the *Education of Cyrus* (Κύρου παιδεία) we have Xenophon's scheme for a perfect education. Despite the scene in which it is laid, it is purely Hellenic, made up of Athenian and Spartan elements in about equal proportions. For this reason also it has a special interest for us. As the portion of the treatise dealing directly with public education is brief, we can hardly do better than transcribe it in a translation.

"Cyrus is still celebrated in legend and song by the barbarians as a man of extraordinary personal beauty, and as of a most gentle, studious, and honor-loving disposition, which made him ready to undergo any labor, and brave any danger, for the sake of praise. Such is the account that has been handed down of his appearance and disposition. He was, of course, educated in accordance with the laws of the Persians. These laws seem to begin their efforts for the public weal at a different point from those of most other states; for most states, after allowing parents to educate their children as they please, and the older people even to spend their time according to their own preference, lay down such laws as: Thou shalt not steal, Thou shalt not rob, Thou shalt not commit burglary, Thou shalt not commit assault, Thou shalt not commit adultery, Thou shalt not disobey a magistrate, etc.; and if any one transgresses any of these laws, they inflict punishment on him. The Persian laws, on the contrary, provide beforehand that the citizens shall never, from the very first, have any disposition to commit a wicked or base act. And they do so in this way. They have what they call a Freemen's Square, where the royal palace and the other public buildings stand. From this square are removed all wares and chafferers, with their cries and vulgarities, to another place, so that their din and disorder may not interfere with the decorum of the cultivated class. This square in the neighborhood of the public buildings is divided into four parts, one for boys, one for youths (ἔφηβοι), one for mature men, and one for men beyond the military age. The hour when these shall appear in their places is settled by law. The boys and mature men come at daybreak, the older men when they think fit, except on the special days when they are bound to appear. The youths pass the night by the public buildings in light armor, only those who are married being excused. These are not hunted up, unless they have been ordered beforehand to appear; but it is not thought decent to be often absent. Each of these divisions is under the charge of twelve governors, one from each of the twelve tribes into which the Persians are divided. The governors of the boys are chosen from among the elderly men, with special view to their fitness for making the most of boys, while those of the youths are chosen from among the mature men upon a similar principle. Those of the mature men are selected with a view to their ability to hold these to their regular duties, and to the special commands of the supreme authority. Even the old men have presidents appointed over them, who see that they perform their duty. What the duties of each are we shall now state, in order to show just how provision is made for securing the highest worth on the part of the citizens.

"First, then, the boys, when they go to school, spend their time in learning justice. They say they go for that purpose, just as our boys go to learn letters. Their governors spend the greater part of the day in acting as judges among them. It is needless to say that boys, as well as men, bring charges against each other of theft and robbery and violence and deceit and slander, and similar things, and those whom the judges find guilty of any of these they punish. But they also punish those whom they find bringing false charges. They pronounce judgment likewise on a charge which, more than anything else, makes men hate each other, and for which they are judged less than for any other, namely, ingratitude. If the judges find a boy in a position to return a favor and not doing it, they punish him severely, believing that persons who are ungrateful will, more than any others, be undutiful to the gods, to parents, country, and friends. It is generally held that ingratitude, more than aught else, leads to irreverence, and we need not add that *it* is the prime mover in every form of baseness. They teach the boys also self-denial, and these are greatly aided in learning this virtue from seeing it daily practised by their elders. Another thing they teach them is obedience to those placed in authority over them; and they are greatly aided in learning this, by seeing their elders strictly obeying their governors. Another thing yet which they teach them is self-discipline in matters of eating and drinking; and they are greatly aided in this by seeing that their elders never absent themselves for the purpose of eating, until they are permitted to do so by their governors, as well as by the fact that they (the boys) do not eat with their mothers, but with their teachers, and at a signal from their governors. As food, they bring with them from home bread, as a relish, nasturtium, and in order to drink, if they are thirsty, they bring an earthen cup to draw water from the river with. In addition to all these things, the boys learn to shoot with the bow and to throw the javelin. Up to the age of sixteen or seventeen years, these are the studies in which the boys engage; after that they are transferred to the class of cadets ($\check{\epsilon}\phi\eta\beta\omega$).

"These cadets spend their time in this way: For ten years from the time when they graduate from the boys' class, they sleep, as we have already said, in the precincts of the public buildings, acting at once as a guard to the city and practising self-denial. It is generally agreed, indeed, that this is the age which especially requires attention. During the day they are at the disposal of their governors, and ready to perform any public service required. If no such service is demanded, they remain in the neighborhood of the public buildings. When the king goes out to hunt, which he does many times a month, he takes with him one-half of the tribes, and leaves the other behind. Those youths who accompany him must carry with them bows and, in a sheath alongside their quivers, a bill or scimitar; also a light shield, and two javelins apiece, one to throw, the other to use, if necessary, at close quarters. For this reason they make hunting a matter of public concern, and the king, as in war, acts as their leader, hunts himself, and sees that the others hunt, the Persians being of opinion that this is the best of all preparations for war. And, indeed, it accustoms them to rise early, and to bear heat and cold; it affords them exercise in marching and running, and compels them to use their bows or their javelins upon wild animals, wherever they happen to come upon them. They are often forced, moreover, to sharpen their courage, when they find themselves face to face with some powerful animal. They must, of course, wound the one that comes to close quarters, and hold at bay the one that attacks them. Hence it is difficult to find in war anything that is absent from the chase. When they go out to hunt, the young men, of course, take with them a larger luncheon than the boys are allowed to have; but this is the only difference between the two. And while they are hunting, they sometimes do not lunch at all; but, if they have to remain beyond their time on account of some game, or otherwise, if they wish to prolong the chase, they make a dinner of this lunch, and on the following day continue the hunt till dinner-time, counting the two days one, because they consume only one day's food. And they do this for the sake of practice, so that, if ever they should run short of provisions in war, they may be able to do the same thing. These youths have as a relish what game they capture in the chase, otherwise they have nasturtium. And if any one thinks that they eat without pleasure, when they have only nasturtium with their food, or drink without pleasure, when they drink water, let him remember how sweet barley-cake and wheaten bread are when he is hungry, and how sweet water is when he is thirsty. The tribes that remain behind, when the king goes hunting, spend their time in the same studies which they pursued as boys, including shooting and javelin-casting, and in these continual contests are going on. There are likewise public exhibitions in them, at which prizes are offered; and whichever tribe contains most young men exceptionally proficient, manly, and steady, is commended by the citizens, who likewise honor, not only their present governor, but also the governor who had charge of them as boys. The young men who are left behind are also employed by the authorities, if any such service is required as manning a guard-house, tracking out malefactors, running down robbers, or anything demanding strength and swiftness. Such are the studies of the young men. And when they have passed ten years in these, they graduate into the class of mature men.

"From the date of this graduation, they spend five and twenty years more in the following manner: In the first place, like the young men, they place themselves at the disposal of the authorities for any public service requiring at once sagacity and unimpaired strength. If they are required to take the field in war, men proficient as they are go armed, no longer with bows and javelins, but with what are called hand-to-hand weapons, breast-plates, shields in their left hands, such as we see in pictures of the Persians, and a sword or bill in their right. And all the officials are drawn from this class, except the boys' teachers. And when they have passed twenty-five years in this class, they are something more than fifty years of age. At that age they graduate into the class of elders, as, indeed, they are called.

"These elders no longer serve in war outside their own country, but, remaining at home, act as judges in public and private cases. They do so even in capital cases. They likewise choose all the officials, and if any person belonging to either of the classes of young and mature men neglects any of his lawful duties, the governor of his tribe, or any one else who pleases, may report him to the elders, and these, if they find the fact to be as reported, expel him from his tribe, and he who is expelled remains dishonored all his life.

"To give a clearer notion of the polity of the Persians as a whole, I will retrace my steps a little. After what has been said, this may be done in a very few words: The Persians, then, are said to number about one hundred and twenty thousand. Of these, none is excluded by law from honors or offices; but all Persians are allowed to send their sons to the public schools of justice. However, it is only those who are able to maintain their sons without employment that send them there: the rest do not. On the other hand, those that are educated by the public teachers are permitted to spend their youth among the *ephēboi*, while those who have not completed this education are not. Again those that pass their youth

among the *ephēboi*, and come up to the legal requirements, are allowed to graduate into the class of mature
men, and to participate in honors and offices; whereas
those who do not pass through the grade of the
ephēboi do not rise to the class of mature men. Finally,
those who complete the curriculum of the mature men
without reproach, pass into the class of elders. Thus
it is that this class of elders is composed of men who
have passed through all the grades of culture. Such is
the polity of the Persians, and such is the system of
training whereby they endeavor to secure the highest
worth."

This Utopian scheme of education has a peculiar
interest, because it is nothing more or less than the
old ideal of Greek education become fully conscious of
itself, under the influence of the new ideal. Let us
call attention to the main points of it. (1) The education here set forth is purely political: men are regarded simply and solely as citizens; all honors are
civic honors. (2) No provision is made for the education of women, their range of activity being entirely
confined to the family. (3) Distinction is made to
rest upon education and conduct. (4) The poorer
classes of the population, though not legally excluded
from education, position, and power, are virtually excluded by their poverty, so that the government is
altogether in the hands of the rich, and is, in fact, an
aristocracy, while pretending to be a democracy:
hence, (5) Social distinctions are distinctions of
worth, which is just the Greek ideal.

There is, however, one point in the scheme which
shows that it is reactionary, directed against prevail-

ing tendencies. Not one word is said of the intellectual side of education, of music or letters. It is evident that Xenophon, himself a man of no mean literary attainments, clearly saw the dangers to Greek life and liberty involved in that exaggerated devotion to literary and intellectual pursuits which followed the teaching of the sophists and Socrates, and that, in order to check this perilous tendency, he drew up a scheme of education from which intellectual and literary pursuits are altogether excluded, in which justice takes the place of letters, and music is not mentioned.

This suggests a curious inquiry in respect to his *Memoirs of Socrates*. This work has generally been regarded as giving us a more correct notion of the real, living Socrates than the manifestly idealizing works of Plato. But was not Xenophon, who could not fail to see the future power of Socrates' influence, as anxious as Plato to claim the prophet as the champion of his own views, and does not this fact determine the whole character of his work? Is it not a romance, in the same sense that the *Cyropædia* is, with only this difference, that the facts of Socrates' life, being fairly well known to those for whom Xenophon was writing, could not be treated with the same freedom and disregard as those of Cyrus' life?

Before we part with Xenophon, we must call attention to another treatise of his, in which he deals with a subject that was then pressing for consideration — the education of women. While, as we have seen, the Æolian states and even Dorian Sparta provided, in some degree, for women's education, Athens appar-

ently, conceiving that woman had no duties outside
of the family, left her education entirely to the care
of that institution. The conservative Xenophon does
not depart from this view; but, seeing the moral evils
that were springing from the neglect of women and
their inability to be, in any sense, companions to
their cultured, or over-cultured, husbands, he lays
down in his *Œconomics* a scheme for the education of
the young wife *by her husband*. As this affords us an
admirable insight into the lives of Athenian girls and
women, better, indeed, than can be found elsewhere,
we cannot do better than transcribe the first part of it.
It takes the form of a conversation between Socrates
and a young husband, named Ischomachus (Strong
Fighter), and is reported by the former. Socrates
tells how, seeing Ischomachus sitting at leisure in a
certain portico, he entered into conversation with
him, paid him an acceptable compliment, and inquired
how he came to be nearly always busy out of doors,
seeing that he evidently spent little time in the house.
Ischomachus replies: —

"'As to your inquiry, Socrates, it is true that I
never remain indoors. Nor need I; for my wife is
fully able by herself to manage everything in the
house.' 'This again, Ischomachus,' said I, 'is something that I should like to ask you about, whether it
was you who taught your wife to be a good wife, or
whether she knew all her household duties when you
received her from her father and mother.' 'Well,
Socrates,' said he, 'what do you suppose she knew
when I took her, since she was hardly fifteen when
she came to me, and, during the whole of her life

before that, special care had been taken that she should
see, hear, and ask as little as possible. Indeed, don't
you think I ought to have been satisfied if, when
she came to me, she knew nothing but how to take
wool and turn it into a garment, and had seen nothing
but how tasks in spinning are assigned to maids? As
regards matters connected with eating and drinking,
of course she was extremely well educated when
she came, and this seems to me the chief education,
whether for a man or a woman.' 'In all other matters, Ischomachus,' said I, 'you yourself instructed
your wife, so as to make her an excellent housewife.'
'To be sure,' said he, 'but not until I had first sacri-
ficed, and prayed that I might succeed in teaching her,
and she might succeed in learning, what was best for
both of us.' 'Then,' said I, 'your wife took part in
your sacrifice and in these prayers, did she not?'
'Certainly she did,' said Ischomachus, 'and solemnly
promised to the gods that she would be what she
ought to be, and showed every evidence of a disposition not to neglect what was taught her.' 'But do, I
beseech you, Ischomachus, explain to me,' said I,
'what was the first thing you set about teaching her?
I shall be more interested in hearing you tell that,
than if you told me all about the finest gymnastic or
equestrian exhibition.' And Ischomachus replied:
'What *should* I teach her? As soon as she could be
handled, and was tame enough to converse, I spoke
to her in some such way as this: Tell me, my dear,
have you ever considered why I took *you* as my wife,
and why your parents gave you to me? That it was
not because I could not find any one else to share my

bed, you know as well as I. No, but because I was anxious to find for myself, and your parents were anxious to find for you, the most suitable partner in home and offspring, I selected you, and your parents, it seems, selected me, out of all possible matches. If, then, God shall ever bless us with children, then we will take the greatest care of them, and try to give them the best possible education; for it will prove a blessing to both of us to have the very best of helpers and supports in our old age. But at present we have this as our common home. And all that I have, I pass over to the common stock, and all that you have brought with you, you have added to the same. Nor must we begin to count which of us has contributed the larger number of things, but must realize that whichever of us is the better partner contributes the more valuable things. Then, Socrates, my wife replied, and said: In what way can I coöperate with you? What power have I? Everything rests with you. My mother told me that my only duty was to be dutiful. Assuredly, my dear, said I, and my father told me the same thing. But it is surely the duty of a dutiful husband and a dutiful wife to act so that what they have may be improved to the utmost, and by every fair and lawful means increased to the utmost. And what do you find, said my wife, that I can do towards helping you to build up our house? Dear me! said I, whatever things the gods have endowed you with the power to do, and the law permits, try to do these to the best of your ability. And what *are* these? said she. It strikes me, said I, that they are by no means the least important things, unless it be true that in the hive the queen-bee is entrusted with the least important functions. Indeed, it seems to me, my dear, I continued, that the very gods have yoked together this couple called male and female with a very definite purpose, viz. to be the source of the greatest mutual good to the yoke-fellows. In the first place, this union exists in order that living species may not die out, but be preserved by propagation; in the second, the partners in this union, at least in the case of human beings, obtain through it the supports of their old age. Moreover, human beings do not live, like animals, in the open air, but obviously require roofs. And I am sure, people who are going to have anything to bring under a roof must have some one to do outdoor duties; for, you see, ploughing, sowing, planting, herding, are all outdoor employments, and it is from them that we obtain all our supplies. On the other hand, when the supplies have all been brought under cover, there is needed some one to take care of them, and to perform those duties which must be done indoors. Among these are the rearing of children and the preparation of food from the produce of the earth; likewise the making of cloth out of wool. And, since both these classes of duties, the outdoor and the indoor, require labor and care, it seems to me, I said, that God has constructed the nature of woman with a special view to indoor employments and cares, and that of man with a view to outdoor employments and cares. For he has made both the body and the soul of the man better able than those of the woman to bear cold, heat, travelling, military service, and so has assigned to him the outdoor employments. And, since he has made the body of woman less able to endure these things, he seems to me to have assigned to her the indoor employments. Considering, moreover, that he had made it woman's nature and duty to nourish young children, he imparted to her a greater love for babies than he did to man. And, inasmuch as he had made it part of woman's duty to take care of the income of the family, God, knowing that for care-taking the soul is none the worse for being ready to fear, bestowed upon woman a greater share of fear than upon a man. On the other hand, knowing that he who attends to the outdoor employments will have to protect the family from wrong-doers, he endowed him with a greater share of courage. And, since both have to give and receive, he divided memory and carefulness between them, so that it would be difficult to determine which of the sexes, the male or the female, is the better equipped with these. And the necessary self-denial he divided between them, and made a decree that, whichever of the two, the husband or the wife, was the superior, should be rewarded with the larger share of this blessing. And just because the nature of man and the nature of woman are not both equally fitted for all tasks, the two are the more dependent upon each other, and their union is the more beneficial to them, because the one is able to supply what the other lacks. And now, said I, my dear, that we know the duties which God has assigned to us respectively, it becomes each of us to do our best, in order to perform these duties. And the law, I continued, coincides with the divine

intention, and unites man and woman. And, just as
God has made them partners in offspring, so the law
makes them partners in the household. And the law
sets its approval upon that difference of function
which God has signified by the difference of ability
which marks the sexes. For it is more respectable
for a woman to remain indoors than to spend her time
out of doors, and less respectable for a man to remain
indoors than to attend to outdoor concerns. And, if
any one acts in a manner at variance with this divine
ordination, it may be that his transgression does not
escape the notice of the gods, and that he is punished
for neglecting his own duties or performing those of
his wife. It appears to me, said I, that the queen-
bee also performs duties that are assigned to her by
God. And what duties, said my wife, does the queen-
bee perform, that have any resemblance to those
incumbent upon me? This, said I, that she remains
in the hive and does not allow the other bees to be
idle, but sends out those that have to work to their
business, and knows and receives what each brings
in, and takes care of it till it is needed for use. And
when the time for using comes, she distributes to each
her just share. Besides this, she attends to the con-
struction of the honey-combs that goes on indoors,
and sees that it is done properly and rapidly, and
carefully sees that the young swarm is properly
reared. And when it is old enough, and the young
bees are fit for work, she sends them out, as a colony,
under the leadership of one of the old ones. And
will it be my duty, said my wife, to do these things?
Exactly so, said I, it will be your duty to remain

indoors, to send out together to their work those
whose duties lie out of doors, and to superintend those
who have to work indoors, to receive whatever is
brought in, to dispense whatever has to be paid out,
while the necessary surplus you must provide for, and
take care that the year's allowance be not spent in a
month. When wool is brought in to you, you must
see that it is turned into cloth; and when dried grain
comes, that it is properly prepared for food. There
is, however, one of your duties, said I, that will
perhaps seem somewhat disagreeable to you. Whenever any one of the slaves is sick, you will have to
see that he is properly nursed, no matter who he is.
Indeed, said my wife, that will be a most pleasant
duty, if those who have been carefully nursed are going to be grateful and kindlier than they were before.
And I,' said Ischomachus, 'admiring her answer, continued: Don't you suppose, my dear, that by such
examples of care on the part of the queen of the hive
the bees are so disposed to her that, when she leaves,
none of them are willing to remain behind, but all
follow her? And my wife replied: I should be sur-
prised if the duties of headship did not fall to you
rather than to me. For my guardianship and disposal
of things in the house would be ridiculous, unless you
saw to it that something was brought in from without.
And my bringing-in would be ridiculous, said I, if
there were no one to take care of what I brought?
Don't you see, I said, how those who pour water into a
leaky barrel, as the expression is, are pitied, as wast-
ing their labour? And indeed, said my wife, they are
to be pitied, if they do that. There are other special

duties, said I, that are sure to become pleasant to
you; for example, when you take a raw hand at
weaving and turn her into an adept, and so double
her value to you, or when you take a raw hand at
managing and waiting and make her capable, reliable,
and serviceable, so that she acquires untold value, or
when you have it in your power to reward those male
slaves that are dutiful and useful to your family, or
to punish one who proves the opposite of this. But
the pleasantest thing of all will be, if you prove
superior to me, and make me your knight, and if you
need not-fear that, as you advance in years, you will
forfeit respect in the house, but are sure that, as you
grow older, the better a partner you are to me, and
the better a mother to the children, the more highly
you will be respected in the house. For all that is
fair and good, said I, increases for men, as life
advances, not through beauties, but through virtues.
Such, Socrates, to the best of my recollection, was the
first conversation I had with my wife.' "

Ischomachus goes on and tells how, in subsequent
conversations, he taught his wife the value of order,
" how to have a place for everything, and everything
in its place," how to train a servant, and how to
make herself attractive without the use of cosmetics
or fine clothes. But enough has been quoted to show
what the ideal family relation among the Athenians
was, and what education was thought fitting for girls
and women. Just as the man was merged in the
citizen, so the woman was merged in the housewife,
and they each received the education and training
demanded by their respective duties. If Athenian

husbands had all been like Ischomachus, it is clear
that the lives of wives might have been very happy
and useful, and that harmony might have reigned in
the family.   But, unfortunately, that was not very
often the case.   Wives, being neglected, became lazy,
wasteful, self-indulgent, shrewish, and useless, while
their husbands, finding them so, sought in immoral
relations with brilliant and cultivated *hetœræ,* or in
worse relations still, a coarse substitute for that satisfaction which they ought to have sought and found in
their own homes.   Thus there grew up a condition of
things which could not fail to sap the moral foundations of society, and which made thoughtful men turn
their attention to the question of woman's education
and sphere of duty.

CHAPTER III

PLATO

All human laws are nourished by the one divine law; for it prevaileth as far as it listeth, and sufficeth for all and surviveth all. — HERACLITUS.

Though reason is universal, the mass of men live as if they had each a private wisdom of his own. — *Id.*

ANTIGONE.   . . . But him will I inter;
         And sweet 't will be to die in such a deed,
         And sweet will be my rest with him, the sweet,
         When I have righteously offended here.
         For longer time, methinks, have I to please
         The dwellers in yon world than those in this;
         For I shall rest forever there. But thou,
         Dishonor still what's honored of the gods.
                    — SOPHOCLES, *Antigone.*

The circle that gathered round Isaiah and his household in these evil days, holding themselves apart from their countrymen, treasuring the word of revelation, and waiting for Jehovah, were indeed, as Isaiah describes them, "signs and tokens in Israel from Jehovah of hosts that dwelleth in Mount Zion." The formation of this little community was a new thing in the history of religion. Till then no one had dreamed of a fellowship of faith dissociated from all national forms, maintained without the exercise of ritual services, bound together by faith in the divine word alone. It was the birth of a new era in the Old Testament religion, for it was the birth of the conception of the *Church*, the first step in the emancipation of spiritual religion from the forms of political life, — a step not less significant that all its consequences were not seen till centuries had passed away. — W. ROBERTSON SMITH, *Prophets of Israel.*

Still at the prophets' feet the nations sit. — LOWELL.

That which is to be known I shall declare, knowing which a man attains immortality — the beginningless Supreme Brahma that is said to be neither Aught nor Naught. — *Bhagavad Gîtâ.*

The only Metaphysics which really and immediately sustains Ethics is one which is itself primarily ethical, and made of the stuff of Ethics. — SCHOPENHAUER.

IN answer to the burning question, How can Athens be brought back to moral life and strength? Socrates had answered, "By finding a new moral sanction." He had even gone further, and said: "This sanction is to be found in correct thinking, in thinking whole thoughts, which, because they are whole, are absolutely true, being the very principles according to which God governs the world." This is, obviously, a mere formal answer. If it was to be of any real service, three further questions had to be answered: (1) How can whole thoughts be reached? (2) What do they prove to be when they are reached? (3) How can they be applied to the moral reorganization of human life? Plato's philosophy is but an attempt to answer these questions. It therefore naturally falls into three divisions, (1) *Dialectics,* including Logic and Theory of Knowledge, (2) *Theoretics,* including Metaphysics and Physics, (3) *Practics,* including Ethics and Politics.

It is obvious that any attempt to reform society on Socratic principles must proceed, not from society itself, but from some person or persons in whom these principles are realized, and who act upon it from without. These persons will be the philosophers or, rather, the sages. Two distinct questions, therefore, present themselves at the outset: (1) How does a man become a sage? (2) How can the sage organize human life, and secure a succession of sages to continue his work after him? To the first of these questions, dialectics gives the answer; to the second, practics; while theoretics exhibits to us at once the origin and the end, that is, the meaning, of all existence, the human included. In the teaching of Plato we find, for the first time recognized and exhibited, the extra-civic or super-civic man, the man who is not a mere fragment of a social whole, completely subordinated to it, but who, standing above society, moulds it in accordance with ideas derived from a higher source. Forecasts of this man, indeed, we find in all Greek literature from Homer down, — in Heraclitus, Sophocles, etc., and especially, as we have seen, in Pythagoras; — but it is now for the first time that he finds full expression, and tries to play a conscious part. In him we have the promise of the future Church.

But to return to the first of our two questions, How does a man become a sage? We found the answer to be, By the dialectic method. Of this, however, not all men have the inclination to avail themselves, but only a chosen few, to whom the gods have granted the inspiration of Love (ἔρως) — a longing akin to madness (μανία), kindled by physical beauty, but tending to the Supreme Good. This good, as we shall see, consists in the vision (θεωρία) of eternal truth, of being, as it is. The few men who are blessed with this love are the divinely appointed reformers and guides of mankind, the well-being of which depends upon submission to them. The dialectic method is the process by which the inspired mind rises from the beauty of physical things, which are always particulars, to the beauty of spiritual things, which are always universals, and finally to the beauty of the Supreme Good, which is *The Universal*. The man who has reached this last, and who sees its relation to all other universals, so that they form together a correlated whole, sees all truth, and is the sage. What we call universals Plato called "ideas" ($\imath\delta\acute{\epsilon}\alpha\iota$ = forms or species). These ideas he regards as genera, as numbers, as active powers, and as substances, the highest of which is God.

Two things are especially notable in connection with this theory: (1) that it involves that Oriental ascetic view of life which makes men turn away from the sensible world, and seek their end and happiness in the colorless world of thought; (2) that it suggests a view of the nature of God which comes perilously near to Oriental pantheism. Plato, indeed, nowhere denies personality of God; but neither does he affirm it, and he certainly leaves the impression that the Supreme Being is a force acting according to a numerical ratio or law. It would be difficult to overestimate the influence of these two views upon the subsequent course of Greek education and life. The former suggested to the super-civic man a sphere of activity which he could flatter himself was superior to the civic, viz. a sphere of contemplation; while the second, by blurring, or rather ignoring, the essential elements of personality in God, viz. consciousness, choice, and will, left no place for a truly religious or moral life. This explains why Platonism, while it has inspired no great civic movement, has played such a determining part in ecclesiasticism, and why, nevertheless, the Church for ages was compelled to fight the tendencies of it, which it did in great measure under the ægis of Plato's stern critic, Aristotle.

We are now ready to take up our second question: How can the sage organize human life, and secure a succession of sages to continue his work after him? Plato has given two widely different answers to this question, in his two most extensive works, (1) the *Republic*, written in his earlier life, when he was under the influence of Heraclitus, Parmenides, and Socrates, and stood in a negative attitude toward the real world of history, (2) the *Laws*, written toward the end of his life, when he became reconciled, in part at least, to the real world and its traditional beliefs, and found satisfaction and inspiration in the teachings of Pythagoras. His change of allegiance is shown by the fact that in the *Laws*, and in them alone, Socrates does not appear as a character. We shall speak first of the *Republic*, and then point out wherein the *Laws* differs from it.

When Plato wrote his *Republic*, he was deeply impressed with the evils and dangers of the social order in which he lived. This impression, which was that of every serious man of the time, had in his case probably been deepened by the teaching and the tragic death of Socrates. The dangers were, obviously, the demoralization of Athenian men and women, and the consequent weakening and dissolution of the social bonds. The evils, as he saw them, were (1) the defective education of children, (2) the neglect of women, (3) the general disorganization of the State through individualism, which placed power in the hands of ignorance and rapacity, instead of in those of wisdom and worth. The *Republic* is a scheme for removing these evils and averting the consequent dangers. It is the Platonic sage's recipe for the healing of society, and it is but fair to say that, of all the Utopian and æsthetic schemes ever proposed for this end, it is incomparably the best. It proposes nothing less than the complete transformation of society, without offering any hint as to how a selfish and degraded people is to be induced to submit thereto. In the transformed society, the State is all in all; the family is abolished; women are emancipated and share in the education and duties of men; the State attends to the procreation and education of children; private property is forbidden. The State is but the individual writ large, and the individual has three faculties, in the proper development and coördination of which consists his well-being: the same, therefore, must be true of the State. These faculties are (1) intellect or reason, (λογιστικόν, λόγος, νοῦς, etc.), (2) spirit or courage (θυμός, θυμοειδές), (3) desire or appetite (ἐπιθυμία, ἐπιθυμητικόν, φιλοχρήματον). The first resides in the head, the second in the heart, the third in the abdomen. The first is peculiar to man, the second he shares with the animals, and the third with both animals and plants. The proper relation of these faculties exists when reason, with clear insight, rules the whole man (Prudence); when spirit takes its directions from reason in its attitude toward pleasure and pain (Fortitude); when spirit and appetite together come to an understanding with reason as to when the one, and when the other, shall act (Temperance); and, finally, when each of the three strictly confines itself to its proper function (Justice). Thus we obtain the four "cardinal virtues." As existing in the individual, they are relations between his own faculties. It is only in the State that they are relations between the individual and his fellows. Rather we ought to say, they are relations between different classes of society; for society is divided into three classes, marked by the predominance of one or other of the three faculties of the soul. *First*, there is the intelligent class, — the philosophers or sages; *second*, the spirited class, — the military men or soldiers; *third*, the covetous class, — men devoted to industry, trade, and money-making. The well-being of the State, as of the individual, is secure only when the relations between these classes are the four cardinal virtues; when the sages rule, and the soldiers and money-makers accept this rule, and when each class strictly confines itself to its own function, so, for example, that the sages do not attempt to fight, the soldiers to make money, or the money-makers to fight or rule. In the Platonic ideal State, accordingly, the three classes dwell apart and have distinct functions. All the power is in the hands of the philosophers, who dwell in lofty isolation, devoted to the contemplation of divine ideas, and descending only through grace to mingle with human affairs, as teachers and absolute rulers, ruling without laws. Their will is enforced by the military class, composed of both sexes, which lives outside the city, devoting itself to physical exercises and the defence of the State. These two classes together con-

stitute the guardians (φύλακες) of the State, and stand
to each other in the relation of head and hand. They
produce nothing, own nothing, live sparingly, and,
indeed, cherish a sovereign contempt for all producing
and owning, as well as for those who produce and own.
They find their satisfaction in the performance of their
functions, and the maintenance of virtue in the State.
What small amount of material good they require is
supplied to them by the industrial class, which they
protect in the enjoyment of the only good it strives
after or can appreciate, the good of the appetites.
This class, of course, has no power, either directive
or executive, being incapable of any. It is, nevertheless, entirely happy in its condition of tutelage,
and, as far as virtue can be predicated of sensuality,
virtuous, the excesses of sensuality being repressed by
the other two classes. Indeed, the great merit which
Plato claims for his scheme is, that it secures harmony,
and therefore happiness, for all, by placing every individual citizen in the class to which by nature he belongs, that is, in which his nature can find the fullest
and freëst expression compatible with the well-being
of the whole. Such is Plato's political scheme, marked
by the two notorious Greek characteristics, love of
harmony and contempt for labor. It is curious to
think that it foreshadowed three modern institutions
— the ecclesiastical hierarchy, the standing army, and
the industrial community, in which, however, the
relations of power demanded by Plato are almost
reversed, with (it is only fair to say) the result
which he foresaw.

In trying to answer the question, By what means

shall these classes be sundered? Plato calmly assumes that his scheme is already in full operation among grown people, so that the only difficulty remaining is with regard to the children. And this is completely met by his scheme of education. The State or, let us say at once, the philosophic class, having abolished the family, and assumed its functions, determines what number and kind of children it requires at any given time, and provides for them as it would for sheep or kine. It brings together at festivals the vigorous males and females, and allows them to choose their mates for the occasion. As soon as the children are born, they are removed from their mothers and taken charge of in State institutions, where the feeble and deformed are at once destroyed. Any children begotten without the authority of the State share the same fate, either before or after birth. Those whose birth is authorized, and who prove vigorous, are reared by the State, none of them knowing, or being known by, their parents. But they by no means suffer any diminution of parentage on that account; for every mature man regards himself as the father, and every mature woman regards herself as the mother, of all the children born within a certain time, so that every child has thousands of fathers and mothers, all interested in his welfare; and the mothers, being relieved from nearly all the duties of maternity, share equally with the men in all the functions of the State.

The system of education to which the children of the State are subjected is, to a large extent, modelled after that of Sparta, especially in respect to its rigor and its absolutely political character. It contains, however, a strong Ionic or Athenian element, notably on the intellectual and æsthetic side. It may fairly claim to be intensely Hellenic. It accepts the time-honored division of education into Music and Gymnastics, making no distinct place for Letters, but including them under Music. It demands that these two branches shall be pursued as parts of a whole, calculated to develop, as far as may be, the harmonious human being, and fit him to become part of the harmonious State. I have said "as far as may be," because Plato believes that only a small number of persons at any given time can be reduced to complete harmony. These are the born philosophers, who, when their nature is fully realized, no longer require the State, but stand, as gods, above it. In truth, the State is needed just because the mass of mankind cannot attain inner harmony, but would perish, were it not for the outer harmony imposed by the philosophers. This is a sad fact, and would be altogether disheartening, were it not for the belief, which Plato seems to have derived from Pythagoras and the Egyptians, that those human beings who fail to attain harmony in one life, will have opportunities to do so in other lives, so long as they do not, by some awful and malignant crime or crimes, show that they are utterly incapable of harmony. Plato's scheme of political education, therefore, requires, as its complement, the doctrines of individual immortality, of probation continued through as many lives as may be necessary, and of the possibility of final and eternal blessedness or misery. In fact, Plato has a fully-developed eschatology, with an "other world," consisting of three well-defined parts,— Elysium, Acheron, and Tartarus, — corresponding to the Paradise, Purgatory, and Hell of Catholic Christianity; with one important difference, however, due to the doctrine of metempsychosis. While the Christian purgatory is a place or state of purgation for souls whose probation is over forever, Acheron is merely a place where imperfect souls remain till the end of a world-period, or æon, of ten thousand years, when they are again allowed to return to life and renew their struggle for that complete harmony which is the condition of admission to the society of the gods.

It is from this eschatology that Plato derives the moral sanctions which he employs in his State. It is true that no one has insisted with greater force than he upon the truth that virtue is, in and for itself, the highest human good; he believed, however, that this could be appreciated only by the philosopher, who had experience of it, and that for the lower orders of men a more powerful, though less noble, sanction was necessary. Accordingly, he depicts the joys of Elysium in images that could not but appeal to the Hellenic imagination, and paints Tartarus in gruesome colors that would do honor to a St. Ignatius.

In order fully to understand the method of Plato's political education, we must revert to Chapter III of Book I. There we saw that, according to the Greeks, a complete education demanded three things, (1) a noble nature, (2) training through habit, (3) instruction. For the first Plato would do what can be done by artificial selection of parents; for the second, he would depend upon music and gymnastics; for the third, upon philosophy. In these last two divisions we have the root of the mediæval *trivium* and *quadrivium*. The Platonic pedagogical system seeks to separate the ignoble from the noble natures, and to place the former in the lowest class. It then trains the noble natures in music and gymnastics, and, while this is going on, it tries to distinguish those natures which are capable of rising above mere training to reflective or philosophic thought, from those which are not. The latter it assigns to the military class, which always remains at the stage of training, while the former are instructed in philosophy, and, if they prove themselves adepts, are finally admitted to the ruling class, as sages. Any member of either of the higher classes who proves himself unworthy of that class, may at any time be degraded into the next below.

As soon as the children are accepted by the State, their education under State nurses begins. The chief efforts of these for some time are directed to the bodies of the children, to seeing that they are healthy and strong. As soon as the young creatures can stand and walk, they are taught to exert themselves in an orderly way and to play little games; and as soon as they understand what is said to them, they are told stories and sung to. Such is their first introduction to gymnastics and music. What games are to be taught, what stories told, and what airs sung to the children, the State determines, and indeed, since the character of human beings depends, in great measure, upon the first impression made upon them, this is one of its most sacred duties. Plato altogether disapproves of leaving children without guidance to seek exercise and amusement in their own way, and demands that their games shall be such as call forth, in a gentle and harmonious way, all the latent powers of body and mind, and develop the sense of order, beauty, and fitness. He is still more earnest in insisting that the stories told to children shall be exemplifications of the loftiest morality, and the airs sung to them such as settle, strengthen, and solemnize the soul. He follows Heraclitus in demanding that the Homeric poems, so long the storehouse for children's stories, shall be entirely proscribed, on account of the false ideals which they hold up both of gods and heroes, and the intimidating descriptions which they give of the other world. Virtue, he holds, cannot be furthered by fear, which is characteristic only of slaves. He thinks that all early intellectual training should be a sort of play. The truth is, the infant-school of Plato's *Republic* comes as near as can well be imagined to the ideal of the modern kindergarten.

While this elementary education is going on, the officers of the State have abundant opportunity for observing the different characters of the children, and distinguishing the noble from the ignoble. As soon as a child shows plainly that it belongs by nature to the lowest class, they consign it to that class, and its education by the State practically ceases. Of course these officers know from what class each child came, and they make use of this knowledge in determining its future destiny. At the same time, they are not to be entirely guided by it, but to act impartially.

The education of the lowest class after childhood the State leaves to take care of itself, persuaded that appetite will always find means for its own satisfaction. The nobler natures it continues to educate, without any break, until they reach the age of twenty. And this education is distinctly a military training. As time goes on, the gymnastic exercises become more violent, more complex, and more sustained, but always have for their subject the soul, rather than the body, and never degenerate into mere athletic brutality. Special attention is directed to the musical and literary exercises, as the means whereby the soul is directly trained and harmonized. Plato holds that no change can be made in the "music" of a State, without a corresponding change in the whole organization; in other words, that the social and political condition of a people is determined by the literature and music which it produces and enjoys. He virtually says, Let me make the songs of a people, and he who will may make their laws. Of the character of the music which he recommends we have already spoken. From literature he would exclude all that we are in the habit of calling by that name, all that is mimetic, poetic, or creative, and confine the term to what is scientific, didactic, and edifying. He sends the poets out of the State with mock-reverent politeness, as creatures too divine for human use. He is particularly severe upon the dramatists, not sparing even the sublime Æschylus. In fact, he would banish from his State all art not directly edifying. The literature which he recommends is plainly of the nature of Æsop's *Fables*, the Pythagorean *Golden Words*, and

the Parmenidean or Heraclitean work *On Nature.* If
we wished to express his intent in strictly modern
language, we should have to say that he desired to
replace literary training by ethical and scientific, and
the poetical mode of presenting ideals by the prosaic.
The true music, he held, is in the human being. "If
we find," he says, "a man who perfectly combines
gymnastics with music, and in exact proportion
applies them to the soul, we shall be entirely justified in calling him the perfect musician and the
perfect trainer, far superior to the man who arranges
strings alongside each other."

There are many matters of detail in Plato's scheme
of military training that well deserve consideration,
but cannot be even touched upon here. Before we
leave it, however, we may give the dates at which the
different branches of education are to begin. Care
of the body begins at birth, story-telling with the
third year, gymnastics with the seventh, writing and
reading with the tenth, letters and music with the
fourteenth, mathematics with the sixteenth, military
drill, which for the time supplants all other training,
with the eighteenth. When the young people reach
the age of twenty, those who show no great capacity
for science, but are manly and courageous, are assigned
to the soldier class, and start on a course of higher
education in military training, while those who evince
great intellectual ability become novices in the ruling
class, and begin a curriculum in science, which lasts
till the close of their thirtieth year. This course
includes arithmetic, geometry, and astronomy, the
only sciences at that time cultivated, and aims at

impressing upon the youthful mind the unity and
harmony of the physical or phenomenal universe. At
the age of thirty, those students who do not show any
particular aptitude for higher studies are drafted off
into the lower public offices, while those who do,
pass five years in the study of dialectics, whereby
they rise to pure ideas. They are then, from their
thirty-fifth to their fiftieth year, made to fill the
higher public offices, in which they take their orders
directly from the sages. During this period they put
their acquirements to a practical test, and so come
really and fully into possession of them. At the end
of their fiftieth year, after half a century of contin-
uous education of body, mind, and will, they are
reckoned to have reached the vision of the supreme
good, and therefore to be fit to enter the contemplative
ruling class. They are now free men; they have
reached the goal of existence; their life is hidden
with God; they are free from the prison of the body,
and only remain in it voluntarily, and out of gratitude
to the State which has educated them, in order to
direct it, in accordance with absolute truth and right,
toward the Supreme Good.

Such, in its outlines, is Plato's theory of education,
as set forth in the *Republic*. It is easy to point out
its defects and its errors, which are neither small nor
few, but fundamental and all-pervasive. But it is
equally easy to see how it came to have these defects
and errors, since they are simply those of every
æsthetic social scheme which ignores the nature of
the material with which it presumes to deal, and
takes no account of the actual history of social insti-

tutions or of the forces by which they are evolved. It is emphatically the product of a youthful intellect, carried away by an artistic ideal. It was, however, the intellect of a Plato, who, when he became more mature, saw, without "irreverence for the dreams of youth," the feebleness of ideas for the conflict with human frailties, and strove to correct his exaggerated estimate of their power.

This he did in the *Laws,* whose very title suggests, in a way almost obtrusive, the change of attitude and allegiance. While in the *Republic* the State is governed by sages, almost entirely without laws, in the later work, the sages almost disappear and the laws assume an all-important place. In writing the *Laws,* moreover, he exchanges allegiance to Socrates and ideas for allegiance to Pythagoras and the gods. In saying this, I have marked the fundamental difference between the *Republic* and the *Laws.* While in the former Plato finds the moral sanctions, in the last resort, in the ideas of the pure intellect, trained in mathematics, astronomy, and dialectics, in the latter he derives them from the content of the popular consciousness, with its gods, its ethical notions, its traditions. In these, as embodied in institutions, he finds the most serviceable, if not the most exalted, revelation of divine truth. Trusting to this, he no longer seeks to abolish the family and private property, but merely to have them regulated; he no longer banishes strangers and poets from his State, but merely subjects them to State supervision; he no longer demands a philosophical training for the rulers, but only practical insight; he no longer divides his citizens into sages, soldiers, and wealth-producers, but into freemen (corresponding to his previous military class) and slaves. His government is no longer an aristocracy of intellect, but a compound of aristocracy, oligarchy, and democracy, representing, respectively, worth, wealth, and will. His plan of education is modified to suit these altered conditions. The children, as in Sparta, do not begin the State course of education until about their seventh year, after which their training is very much the same as that demanded in the *Republic*, with the omission, of course, of dialectics. Though women are no longer to be relieved of their home duties, they are still to share in the education and occupations of men, an arrangement which is facilitated by the law ordaining that both men and women shall eat at public tables. In making these changes, Plato believed that he was falling from a lofty, but unrealizable, ideal, and making concessions to human weakness; in reality, he was approaching truth and right.

Book III

ARISTOTLE (B.C. 384–322)

CHAPTER I

ARISTOTLE — LIFE AND WORKS

Aristotle, in my opinion, stands almost alone in philosophy. — CICERO.

Aristotle, Nature's private secretary, dipping his pen in intellect. — EUSEBIUS.

Wherever the divine wisdom of Aristotle has opened its mouth, the wisdom of others, it seems to me, is to be disregarded. — DANTE.

I could soon get over Aristotle's *prestige*, if I could only get over his reasons. — LESSING.

If, now in my quiet days, I had youthful faculties at my command, I should devote myself to Greek, in spite of all the difficulties I know. Nature and Aristotle should be my sole study. It is beyond all conception what that man espied, saw, beheld, remarked, observed. To be sure he was sometimes hasty in his explanations; but are we not so, even to the present day? — GOETHE (at 78).

If the proper earnestness prevailed in philosophy, nothing would be more worthy of establishing than a foundation for a special lectureship on Aristotle; for he is, of all the ancients, the most worthy of study. — HEGEL.

Aristotle was one of the richest and most comprehensive geniuses that ever appeared — a man beside whom no age has an equal to place. — *Id*.

Physical philosophy occupies itself with the general qualities of matter. It is an abstraction from the dynamic manifestations of the different kinds of matter; and even where its foundations were first laid, in the eight books of Aristotle's *Physical Lectures*, all the phenomena of nature are represented as the motive vital activity of a universal world-force. — ALEXANDER VON HUMBOLDT.

153

It was characteristic of this extraordinary genius to work at both ends of the scientific process. He was alike a devotee to facts and a master of the highest abstractions.   ALEXANDER BAIN.

Aristotle is the *Father of the Inductive Method*, and he is so for two reasons: First, he theoretically recognized its essential principles with a clearness, and exhibited them with a conviction, which strike the modern man with amazement; and then he made the first comprehensive attempt to apply them to all the science of the Greeks. — WILHELM ONCKEN.

Aristotle, for whose political philosophy our admiration rises, the more we consider the work of his successors, is less guided by imagination than Plato, examines reality more carefully, and recognizes more acutely, the needs of man. — BLUNTSCHLI.

It appears to me that there can be no question, that Aristotle stands forth, not only as the greatest figure in antiquity, but as the greatest intellect that has ever appeared upon the face of this earth. — GEORGE J. ROMANES.

Aristotle, with all the wisdom of Plato before him, which he was well able to appropriate, could find no better definition of the true good of man than the full exercise or realization of the soul's faculties in accordance with its proper excellence, which was excellence of thought, speculative and practical. — THOMAS HILL GREEN.

IT is pretty definitely settled, among men competent to form a judgment, that Aristotle was the best educated man that ever walked on the surface of this earth. He is still, as he was in Dante's time, the "master of those that know." It is, therefore, not without reason that we look to him, not only as the best exponent of ancient education, but as one of the worthiest guides and ensamples in education generally. That we may not lose the advantage of his example, it will be well, before we consider his educational theories, to cast a glance at his life, the process of his development, and his work.

Aristotle was born about B.C. 384, in the Greek colony of Stagira in Thrace, near the borders of Macedonia. His father, Nicomachus, was a physician of good standing, the author of several medical works, and the trusted friend of Amyntas, the Macedonian King. His mother, Phæstis, was descended from the early settlers of the place. It was doubtless under his father's guidance that the boy Aristotle first became interested in those physical studies in which he was destined to do such wonderful work. Losing, however, both his parents at an early age, he came under the charge of Proxenus, of Atarneus, who appears to have done his duty by him. At the age of eighteen he came to Athens for his higher education, and entered the school of Plato in the Academy. Here he remained for nearly twenty years, listening to Plato, and acquiring those vast stores of information which in later life he worked up into lectures and scientific treatises. Nothing escaped him, neither art, science, religion, philosophy, nor politics. He seems, being well off, to have begun early to collect a library, and to aim at encyclopædic knowledge. About his methods of study we know very little; but we hear that at times he assisted Plato in his work and was very careful of his own attire. It is clear that, in course of time, he rose in thought above the teachings of his master, and even rejected the most fundamental of them, the doctrine of self-existent ideas. But he never lost respect for that master, and when the latter died, he retired with Xenocrates, son of the new head of the Academy, to Atarneus, the home of his old guardian Proxenus, and of his fellow-

Academic, Hermias, now king or tyrant of the place. Here he remained for three years, in the closest intimacy with his friend, until the latter was treacherously murdered by the Persians. He then crossed over to Mytilene, taking with him Pythias, Hermias' sister or niece, whom he had married, and to whom he was deeply devoted. He erected in Delphi a statue to his dead friend, and dedicated to him a poem, of which we shall hear more in the sequel. About B.C. 343, when he was over forty years old, he was called to Macedonia, as tutor to Alexander, the thirteen-year-old son of King Philip, and grandson of his own father's old patron, Amyntas. This office he filled for about three years with distinguished success, and it may be safely said that never had so great a tutor so great a pupil. During the latter part of the time, at least, Aristotle and Alexander seem to have lived at Stagira. This town had been captured and destroyed by Philip, and its inhabitants scattered. With the permission of the conqueror, Aristotle reassembled the inhabitants, rebuilt the town, drew up its laws, and laid out near it, at Mieza, in imitation of the Academy, a gymnasium and park, which he called the *Nymphœum*. Hither he appears to have retired with his royal pupil and several other youths who were receiving education along with him, among them Theophrastus and the ill-fated Callisthenes. It was probably here that Aristotle adopted the habit of walking while imparting instruction, a habit which afterwards gave the name to his school. When Alexander, at sixteen, entered his father's army, Aristotle still continued to teach in the Nymphæum, which existed even in Plutarch's time, more than four hundred years afterwards. But this lasted only for about five years; for in 335, when Alexander, who in the previous year had succeeded his murdered father, was preparing to invade Persia, Aristotle moved to Athens. Finding that his old friend, Xenocrates, was director of the school in the Academy, he established himself, as a public teacher or professor, in the Lyceum, the Periclean gymnasium, used chiefly, it should seem, by the lower classes and by foreign residents, of whom he himself was one. As an alien, as the friend of the victorious Macedonians, who three years before had broken the power of Greece at Chæronea, and taken away her autonomy forever, as a rival of the Platonists, and as a wealthy, well-dressed gentleman, he had many enemies and detractors; but his conduct seems to have been so unobjectionable that no formal charge could be brought against him. His very numerous pupils were mostly foreigners, a fact not without its influence on the subsequent course of thought. He divided his days between writing and teaching, taking his physical exercise while engaged in the latter occupation. In the mornings he gave lectures to a narrow circle, in a strictly formal and scientific way, upon the higher branches of science; while in the afternoons he conducted conversations upon more popular themes with a less select audience. The former were called his esoteric, the latter his exoteric, discourses.

It was during his second residence in Athens, in the twelve years from B.C. 335 to 323, that Aristotle composed most of those great works in which he

sought to sum up, in an encyclopædic way, the results
of a life of all-embracing study and thought. He had
been in no haste to put himself on record, and it was
not until he had reached a consistent view of the
world that he ventured to treat, in a definitive way,
any aspect of it. Thus it was that each of his treatises formed part of one great whole of thought. Had
he succeeded in completing his plan, he would have
left to the world a body of science such as, even in
our own day, would look in vain for a peer among the
works of any one man. Unfortunately, his plan was
not completed, and even of the works which he did
write only a portion has come down to us. But
that portion is sufficient to place their author at the
head of all scientific men. Some of his works, for
example, his _Logic, Metaphysics, Ethics,_ and _Politics,_
still occupy the first place in the literature of these
subjects. How a single man could have done all that
he did, and in so many different departments, is almost
inconceivable. No doubt he had helpers, in the shape
of secretaries, learned slaves, and disciples; and it is
certain that he received from his royal pupil munifi-
cent aid, which enabled him to do much, especially
in the directions of physical and political research,
that would have been impossible for a poor man; but,
after all allowances have been made, his achievement
still seems almost miraculous.

During all the years in which Aristotle was thus
engaged, his position at Athens was becoming more
and more insecure. The anti-Macedonian party were
waiting for the first opportunity to rid the city of
him, and were prevented from open attempts at this

only by dread of Alexander's displeasure. Even
when it was known that Aristotle had incurred dis-
favor with his old pupil, they did not venture to
attack him; but in 323, when the news of Alexander's
sudden death made all Greece feel that now the time
had come to get rid forever of the hated Macedonians,
and recover its liberty, they at once gave vent to their
long-cherished hatred. How hard it was to find matter for an accusation against him, is shown by the fact
that they had to go back to his old poem on *Worth*,
written in memory of Hermias (see p. 4), and to
base thereon a charge of impiety — a charge always
easily made, and always sure to arouse strong popular
prejudice. According to Athenian law, the defendant
in any such case might, if he chose, escape punishment by leaving the city any time before the trial;
and Aristotle, not being, like Socrates, a citizen,
could have no ground for refusing to take advantage
of this liberty. Accordingly, with the remark that
he would not voluntarily allow the Athenians to sin
a second time against philosophy, he withdrew to his
country residence at Chalcis in Eubœa, the old home
of his mother's family, to wait till affairs should take
another turn, as, indeed, they soon afterwards did,
when Athens had to open her gates to Antipater.
But, ere that happened, Aristotle was in his grave,
having died in 322, shortly before Demosthenes, of
disease of the stomach, from which he had long suf-
fered. His remains are said to have been carried to
Stagira, where the grateful inhabitants erected an altar
over them and paid divine honors to his memory.
His library and the manuscripts of his works he left

in the hands of Theophrastus, who succeeded him in the Lyceum His will, the text of which has come down to us, bears testimony, along with all else that we know of him, to the nobility, kindliness, and justice of his nature.

CHAPTER II

ARISTOTLE'S PHILOSOPHY

Platon rêvait; Aristote pensait. — ALFRED DE MUSSET.

> Are God and Nature then at strife
> That Nature lends such evil dreams?
>
> — TENNYSON.

There are three Essences. Two of these are sensible; one being eternal, and the other perishable. The latter is admitted by all, in the form, for example, of plants and animals; in regard to the former, or eternal one, we shall have to consider its elements, and see whether they be one or many. The third is immutable [and, therefore, inaccessible to sense], and this some thinkers hold to be transcendent. — ARISTOTLE.

The vision of the divine is what is sweetest and best; and if God always enjoys that vision as we sometimes do, it is wonderful, and if he does so in a yet higher degree, it is more wonderful still. And so even it is. And life belongs to him; for the self-determination of thought is life, and he is self-determination. And his absolute self-determination is the supreme and eternal life. And we call God a living being, eternal, best; so that life and duration, uniform and eternal, belong to God; for this is God. — Id.

We must consider in what way the system of the universe contains the good and the best, whether as something transcendent and self-determined, or as order. Surely in both ways at once, as in an army, for which the good is in order, and is the general, and the latter more than the former. For the general is not due to the order, but the order to the general. — Id.

THE thought of Aristotle differs from that of Plato both in its method and in its results. Plato, reared in the school of Pythagoras, Parmenides, Heraclitus,

161

and Socrates, had, naturally enough, come to look for truth in the supersensual region of mind, and thought he found it in ideas attainable by a process of dialectic within the individual consciousness. He thus came to put forward a doctrine which, despite its ostensible purpose to cement the bonds of society, in reality tended to withdraw men from society altogether and increase the very individualism it was intended to cure. Aristotle, while still in Plato's school, had turned away from this doctrine, and in after-life he never lost an opportunity of combating it. He could point to Plato's *Republic* as a warning example of its logical consequences. But, in doing this, he was prepared to put another doctrine in its place, and he did so on the basis of a profound study of the whole course of Greek thought, mythological and philosophical.

Instead of appealing, like Plato, to the individual consciousness, and trying to discover ultimate truth by bringing its data into harmony among themselves, Aristotle appeals to the historic consciousness, and endeavors to find truth by harmonizing and complementing its data through a further appeal to the outer world, in which these data are realized. He maintains that the truths reached by the dialectic process are merely formal, and therefore empty, — useless in practice, until they have been filled by experience from the storehouse of nature. In consequence of this changed attitude, he sets aside the dialectic process, and substitutes for it the *Method of Induction*, which he was the first man in the world to comprehend, expound, and apply, becoming thus the father of all true science. And he makes a more extensive use of in-

duction than any other man since his time, applying
it in a field in which even now it is hardly supposed
to yield any results, the field of the common consciousness. Indeed, he everywhere begins his search
for concrete truth by examining the historic consciousness, and, having, by a process of induction, discovered and generalized its contents, he turns with these
to nature and, by a second induction, corrects, com-
pletes, and harmonizes them. We might express this
in modern language, by saying that his whole endeavor
is to correct and supplement the imperfect human
consciousness by a continual appeal to the divine
consciousness, *as manifested in the world.* It is the
error of modern investigators that they employ only
one-half of the inductive method, the objective, and
either omit altogether the subjective, or else, like
Plato, apply it only to the individual consciousness.
Hence come the widely divergent results which still
meet us in so many of the sciences, in Politics, Psychology, etc., hence the fact that a great deal of
science, instead of correcting, widening, and harmonizing the common consciousness, stands altogether apart
from it, or even in direct opposition to it. The man
who writes a treatise on Psychology, or on the Soul,
without troubling himself to discover what "Soul"
means in the general consciousness of mankind, and
perhaps setting out with an altogether individual
notion of it, can hardly look for any other result.
Aristotle, true to his method of induction, devotes
one entire book of his *Psychology* to finding out what
"Soul" means in the historic consciousness, unre-
flective as well as reflective. Then, with this meaning,

he goes to nature, seeks by induction to discover what she has to say about it, and abides by her reply. Hence it is that his thought has laid hold upon the world, and influenced it in practical ways, as no other man's thought has ever done. Hence it is that, of all ancient men, he is the one before whom the modern scientist bows with respect.

If we now ask ourselves what was the underlying thought that shaped Aristotle's theory of induction, what was his *Weltanschauung*, we shall find it to be this: The divine intelligence reveals itself subjectively in an historic process in the human consciousness, and objectively[1] in a natural process in the outer world. Truth for man is the harmony of the two revelations. It follows directly from this that the scientist must take impartial account of both. So, for example, if he finds gods in the historical consciousness, and laws or forces in nature, he has no right, like the theologian, to merge the latter in the former, or, like the physicist, to replace the former by the latter. He must retain both till he can bring them into harmony. Only then does he know either.

Such a philosophy as this, instead of drawing men away from the world of nature and history, and confining them to the narrow circle of their own consciousness, of necessity sent them back to that world, as the only means by which any human well-being could be reached. It is for this reason that it has so powerfully affected both social life and science. Neverthe-

[1] I am here using the terms "objective" and "subjective" in their modern acceptation, which almost exactly inverts the ancient usage. See Martineau, *Study of Religion*, vol. i, p. 385, n. 2.

less, we should err greatly, if we supposed that, in Aristotle's view, the divine is nothing more than an immanent idea, working as a force-form in nature, and as a thought-form in mind. He does, indeed, believe that the divine is all this, but not that this is all the divine there is. Over and above the divine which is determined in nature and in man, there is the transcendent Mind, or God, determining himself through himself, and bearing the same relation to the divine that the sun bears to light, the human mind to human thought, the general to the order of his army. Here we are far away from Pantheism, and, though we have not yet risen to a clear conception of personality, we have at the "helm of the universe" a conscious being, the source of law and order. And man, rising above the thought whereby he knows himself through nature, and nature through himself, may enter into the consciousness of God and become a partaker in that life which is "sweetest and best." These are the features of Aristotle's thought which in the thirteenth century made it acceptable to the Christian Church in her struggle against Pantheism, and which paved the way for that higher mysticism of which Thomas Aquinas is the most distinguished exponent — a mysticism which does not, like that of the Neoplatonists and Buddhists, dispense with thought to lose itself in vacancy, but which, rising upon a broad basis of knowledge, pierces the clouds of sense, to find itself in the presence of the most concrete Reality, the inexhaustible source of all thought and all things.

CHAPTER III

ARISTOTLE'S THEORY OF THE STATE

First, then, let us try to enumerate whatever worthy utterances have proceeded from men of the past upon any aspect of the subject, and then, referring to our collections of *Constitutional Histories*, let us seek to arrive at a theory as to what sorts of things preserve and destroy each particular form of government, and see for what reasons some are well, some ill, managed. Succeeding in this, we may, perhaps, the better learn both what is the best form of government, and what arrangements, laws, and customs are best suited to each form. — ARISTOTLE.

Man is a political animal. — *Id.*

The State is prior to the individual. — *Id.*

Without friends no one would choose to live, although he possessed all other blessings. — *Id.*

If happiness be self-determination in accordance with worth, we must conclude that it will be in accordance with the supreme worth, which will be the worth of the noblest part of us. This part, whatever it may be, whether intellect (νοῦς) or something else, that which by nature evidently rules and guides us and has insight into things beautiful and divine, whether it be itself divine, or the divinest part of us, is that whose self-determination, in accordance with its proper worth, will be the perfect happiness. That this consists in the vision of divine things has already been said. . . . This, indeed, is the supreme self-determination, for the reason that intellect is the highest part of us, and that with which it deals is the highest of the knowable. . . . But a life of this sort would be something higher than the human; for he who lived it would not be living as man, but as the subject of something divine. . . . If, then, intellect is something divine in relation to man, the life lived according to it must be divine in relation to human life. Instead, then, of following those who advise us, as being human, to set our

166

thoughts upon human things, and, as being mortals, to set them on mortal things, it is our duty, as far as may be, to act as immortal beings, and do all we can to live in accordance with the supreme part of us. — ARISTOTLE.

Man alone, among all beings, occupies a middle place between things corruptible and things incorruptible. . . . Two ends, therefore, Ineffable Providence has ordained for man: Blessedness in this life, which consists in the exercise of native faculty, and is figured by the Earthly Paradise, and blessedness in the eternal life, which consists in the enjoyment of the vision of God, a thing not to be achieved by any native faculty, unless aided by divine light, and which is to be understood by the Heavenly Paradise. . . . These ends and means would be disregarded by human passion, if men were not restrained in their course by bit and bridle. . . . For this reason man required a double directive, corresponding to this double end. He required the Supreme Pontiff to guide the human race to life eternal, and the Emperor to guide the human race to temporal felicity, in accordance with the teachings of philosophy. . . . The truth with regard to the question whether the authority of the Emperor is derived directly from God or from another, must not be taken so strictly as to mean that the Roman Prince is not, in some respects, subject to the Roman Pontiff, the fact being that this mortal felicity of ours is, in some sense, ordained with a view to immortal felicity. Let Cæsar, therefore, display that reverence for Peter which the first-born son ought to display for his father, so that, being illuminated by his father's grace, he may with greater virtue enlighten the world, which he has been called to govern by Him who is governor of all things, spiritual and temporal. —DANTE.

> O Grace abounding, whence I did presume
> To fix my gaze upon the eternal light
> So far that I consumed my sight therein!
> Within its deeps I saw internalized
> Into one volume, bound with love,
> That which is outered in the universe; —
> Substance and accident, and all their modes,
> As 't were, together merged in such a sort
> That what I mean is but a simple light.
> The universal form of this same knot
> I think I saw, because, when thus I speak,
> I feel that I rejoice with larger joy. — *Id.*

Man's chief end is to glorify God, and to enjoy him forever. —
Westminster Shorter Catechism.

PLATO'S chief purpose, in writing upon education,
had been to suggest a remedy for the social and moral
conditions of his native Athens.   Aristotle has no
such purpose.   He is, in a very deep sense, a cosmopolitan, and writes in the interest of science and universal utility.   His range of vision is not confined to
Athens, or even to Greece (though he is very proud
of being a Greek), but ranges over the whole known
world in time and space.   Unlike Plato, too, who had
been familiar mainly with institutions of the past in
Egypt and Greece, Aristotle is deeply affected by the
tendencies of the future, and, though no one lays
greater stress than he upon the necessity of a knowledge of the past for him who would construct a sound
social theory, he nevertheless declares that the whole
of the past is shaped by something which is in the
future, by the ultimate realization.   This view comes
out in a paradoxical way in his famous saying that
"the State is prior to the individual," by which he
means that it is man's political nature working in him
that makes him an individual, and at the same time
realizes itself in a State.   And this brings us to Aristotle's conception of the State, which we must consider
before taking up his theory of education, for the
reason that to him, as to all the ancient world, education is a function of the State, and is conducted, primarily at least, for the ends of the State.

Before venturing upon a theory of the State, Aristotle, true to his inductive principles, wrote the Constitutional Histories of over two hundred and fifty

different states. One of these, the *Constitutional History of Athens*, has recently been discovered and published (see p. 96). He held that it was only by means of a broad induction, thus rendered possible, that he could discover the idea of the State, that is, its self-realizing form. Employing this method, then, he came to the conclusion that the State is that highest social institution which secures the highest good or happiness of man. Having, in a previous treatise, satisfied himself that this good is Worth ($\grave{a}\rho\epsilon\tau\acute{\eta}$), and worth being in every case the full exercise of characteristic or differentiating faculty, he concludes that, since man's distinguishing faculty is reason, the State is the institution which secures to man the fullest and freëst exercise of this. It follows directly that the State is, simply and solely, the supreme educational institution, the university to which all other institutions are but preparatory. And two more conclusions follow: (1) that states will differ in constitution with the different educational needs of the peoples among whom they exist, and (2) that, since all education is but a preparation for some worthy activity, political education, the life of man as a citizen, is but a preparation for the highest activity, which, because it is highest, must necessarily be an end in itself. This activity, Aristotle argues, can be none other than contemplation, the Vision of the Divine ($\theta\epsilon\omega\rho\acute{\iota}a$).

Results which have moved the world followed logically from this doctrine. Whereas Plato had made provision for a small and select body of super-civic men, and so paved the way for religious monasticism and asceticism, Aristotle maintains that in every civilized man, as such, there is a super-civic part, in fact, a superhuman and divine part, for the complete realization of which all the other parts, and the State wherein they find expression, are but means. Here we have, in embryo, the whole of Dante's theory of the relation of Church and State, a theory which lies at the basis of all modern political effort, however little the fact may be recognized. Here, indeed, we have the whole framework of the *Divine Comedy;* here too we have the doctrine of the Beatific Vision, which for ages shaped and, to a large extent, still shapes, the life of Christendom. Well might Dante claim Aristotle as his master (see p. 153)! Well might the great doctors of the Church speak of him as " *The* Philosopher," and as the "Forerunner of Christ in Things Natural." In vain did Peter Ramus and Luther and Bruno and Bacon depreciate or anathematize him! He is more powerful to-day in thought and life than at any time for the last twenty-two centuries.

It may be asked how far, and in what form, Aristotle conceives the divine life to be possible for man on earth. He answers that, though it cannot be perfectly or continuously realized here, it is in some degree and for certain times attainable (see p. 161). In so far as it is a social life, it is the life of friendship or spiritual love (φιλία), to which he has devoted almost two books of his *Ethics,* books which give us a loftier idea of his personal purity and worth than any other of his extant writings. He insists that friendship is the supreme blessing (see p. 166), and that "whatever a man's being is, or whatever he chooses to live for, in that he wishes to spend his life in the company of his friends." It is even said that Aristotle, while teaching in the Lyceum, gathered about him a knot of noble youths and earnest students, and formed them into a kind of community, with a view to leading a truly spiritual social life.

CHAPTER IV

ARISTOTLE'S PEDAGOGICAL STATE

Nature is the beginning of everything. — ARISTOTLE.

Life is more than meat, and the body than raiment. — JESUS.

The forces of the human passions in us, when completely repressed, become more vehement; but when they are called into action for short time and in the right degree, they enjoy a measured delight, are soothed, and, thence being purged away, cease in a kindly, instead of a violent, way. For this reason, in tragedy and comedy, through being spectators of the passions of others, we still our own passions, render them more moderate, and purge them away; and so, likewise, in the temples, by seeing and hearing base things, we are freed from the injury that would come from the actual practice of them. — JAMBLICHUS.

Care for the body must precede care for the soul; next to care for the body must come care for the appetites; and, last of all, care for the intelligence. We train the appetites for the sake of the intelligence, and the body for the sake of the soul. — ARISTOTLE.

The practice of abortion was one to which few persons in antiquity attached any deep feeling of condemnation. . . . The physiological theory that the fœtus did not become a living creature till the hour of birth had some influence on the judgments passed upon this practice. The death of an unborn child does not appeal very powerfully to the feeling of compassion, and men who had not yet attained any strong sense of the sanctity of human life, who believed that they might regulate their conduct on these matters by utilitarian views, according to the general interest of the community, might very readily conclude that prevention of birth was in many cases an act of mercy. In Greece, Aristotle not only countenanced the practice, but even desired that it should be enforced by law, when population had exceeded certain assigned limits. No law in Greece, or in the Roman Republic, or during the

172

greater part of the Empire, condemned it. . . . The language of the Christians from the very beginning was very different. With unwavering consistency and with the strongest emphasis, they denounced the practice, not simply as inhuman, but as definitely murder. — LECKY, *European Morals.*

Aristotle clearly saw that the strong tendency of the human race to increase, unless corrected by strict and positive laws, was absolutely fatal to every system founded on equality of property; and there cannot surely be a stronger argument against any system of this kind than the necessity of such laws as Aristotle himself proposes. . . . He seems to be fully aware that to encourage the birth of children, without providing properly for their support, is to obtain a very small accession to the population of a country, at the expense of a very great accession of misery. — MALTHUS, *Essay on Population.*

CONSIDERING Aristotle's views with regard to man, his end, and the function of the State, we can have little difficulty in divining the character and method of his educational system. Man is a being endowed with reason; his end is the full realization of this, his sovereign and distinguishing faculty; the State is the means whereby this is accomplished.

Readers of Goethe's *Wilhelm Meister* will remember the description, in the second part, of the Pedagogical Province. Now, Aristotle's State might with entire propriety be called a Pedagogical Province. In trying to describe this State, and the manner in which it discharges its function, it is difficult to know where to begin, for the reason that, taken as a whole, the State is both teacher and pupil. It arranges the whole scheme of education, and is therefore related to it as cause; it is built up by this scheme, and is therefore related to it as effect. It comes, accordingly, both at the beginning and at the end.

It is a university which arranges the entire scheme of education, and is itself its highest grade. I shall try to surmount this difficulty by distinguishing what the State is from what it does, beginning with the former, and ending with the latter.

With regard to what the State is, we have to consider (1) its natural, (2) its social, conditions. The former are climate, and extent, nature, and situation of territory; the latter, number and character of inhabitants, property regulations, distinction of classes, city architecture, mode of life, government, and relations to other states.

Aristotle demands for his State a temperate climate, on the ground that a cold one renders men strong and bold, but dull and stupid, while a hot one renders them intellectual but effeminate. The best climate is one that makes them at once brave and intelligent. The territory must be extensive enough, and fertile enough, to supply its inhabitants with all the material conditions of life in answer to labor which shall rouse, without exhausting, their energies. It must face east or south, and be healthy, well-watered, accessible from land and sea, and easily defensible.

As to the social conditions, Aristotle finds the most important to be the number of citizens. And here two things must be carefully borne in mind. (1) He means by "State" a city with a small territory. This is not, as has been erroneously supposed, his highest social unity. He recognizes clearly the nation (ἔθνος) and the confederacy (συμμαχία); but he holds that they exist merely for material ends, whereas the end of the State is spiritual. (2) He means by "citizen" a politician. A man is a citizen, not because he is born or domiciled in a State, but because he is a sharer in its functions. A State made up of mechanics, no matter how great their number, would be a small State, and one composed of slaves would be no State at all. Thus, in estimating the size of a State, we are to consider the character of its inhabitants, their fitness for political functions, rather than their number. Little Athens was a much larger State than gigantic Persia on the field of Marathon. Aristotle lays down that the number of citizens must be large enough to insure independence, this being essential to a Culture-State, and not too large to be manageable. Besides the citizens, there will necessarily be in the State a very large number of other human beings, slaves, agriculturists, mechanics, sailors — for all these he excludes from citizenship on the ground that they do not make virtue, that is, the realization of reason, the end of their lives. Women, in a sense, are citizens, if they belong to the families of citizens; but their sphere is the family.

With regard to property, Aristotle begins by considering what things it is necessary for. These he finds to be six, three private and three public. The former are food (including clothing and shelter), instruments of production, and arms; the latter are public enterprises (civil and military), religion, and law. These are the "necessaries" (ἀναγκαῖα) of a State, for which it must duly provide. The most important of all is religion, on which he everywhere lays great stress. As to the distribution of property, he propounds a scheme which is half socialistic. All the land is to belong to the State, that is, to the body of the free citizens. It is to be divided into two equal portions, and one set apart for public, the other for private, uses. The revenue from the public part is to go for the support of religion (and law?) and of the public tables, from which no citizen is excluded by poverty. The private part is to be so divided that each citizen shall have one lot near the city, and one near the frontier. This will give him an interest in defending the whole territory. Both parts are to be cultivated by serfs or slaves, part of whom will necessarily belong to the State, and part to private individuals. Land-owning is to be a condition of citizenship, and all citizens are to be forbidden to exercise any form of productive industry. This last rule, it is hoped, will prevent grievous inequalities of wealth, and the evils that flow from them. A modest competency, derived from his estate, is all that any citizen should aim at. Only degraded people, incapable of virtue, will crave for more.

Upon the distinction of classes some light has been already thrown. They are two; the ruling and the ruled. Aristotle holds that this distinction runs through the whole of nature and spirit, that it is fundamental in being itself. It holds between God and the universe, form and matter, soul and body, object and subject, husband and wife, parent and child, master and slave, etc., etc. The ruling class again is sub-divided into two parts, one that thinks and determines (legislators and judges), and one that executes (officials, officers, soldiers); while the ruled is sub-divided into husbandmen, mechanics, and sea-men (sailors, fishermen, etc.). All the members of the ruled class are serfs or public slaves, working, not for themselves, but for their masters. Aristotle holds that they ought to be barbarians of different races, and not Greeks.

The architecture of the city will in some degree correspond to this social division. It will naturally fall into three divisions, military, religious, and civil. First of all, a city must have walls. These should have towers and bastions at proper distances, and be made as attractive as possible. The temples of the gods and the offices of the chief magistrates should, if possible, stand together on a fortified citadel, con-spicuously dominating the entire city. Adjoining this ought to be the Freemen's Square, reserved entirely for the ruling class, and unencumbered by business or wares of any sort. Here ought to stand the gymnasium for the older citizens, who will thus be brought into contact with the magistrates and inspired with "true reverence and freemen's fear." The market-square must be placed so as to be conven-ient for the reception of goods both from sea and land. This comprehends all the civil architecture except the mess-halls, of which we shall better speak in the next paragraph.

The mode of life of the ruling class will necessarily differ widely from that of the ruled. About the latter Aristotle has nothing to say. He hopes for little from that class beyond the possibility of being held in contented subordination. As it has no politi-cal life, all that is left to it is the life of the family.

The ruling class, on the contrary, live to a large extent in public, and on public funds. They exercise in public gymnasia and eat at public tables. The chief magistrates have their mess-hall in the citadel; the priests have theirs close to the temples; the magistrates, who preside over business matters, streets, and markets, have theirs near the market-square, while those who attend to the defences of the city have tables in the towers. When not engaged in public business, the citizens may meet in the Freemen's Square and enjoy an open-air *conversazione*, with music, poetry, and philosophy, in a word, διαγωγή, for which our language has no even approximate equivalent (see p. 33). In proportion as they advance in years, the citizens enjoy more and more διαγωγή, which, indeed, is regarded as the end of life, here and hereafter.

The government is entirely in the hands of the free citizens, the legislative and deliberative power being in those of the elders; the executive power, civil and military, in those of the younger portion. It is curious that, though Aristotle regards this as the best possible arrangement under ordinary circumstances, he nevertheless believes that the happiest condition for a State would be to be governed by some divine or heroic man, far superior to all the others in wisdom and goodness. He plainly considers Pisistratus to have been one such man, and he perhaps hoped that Alexander might be another.

The relations of the pedagogical State to other States are, as far as possible, to be peaceful. Just as all labor is for the sake of rest and διαγωγή, so all war is for the sake of peace; and that State is to be envied which can maintain an honorable independence without war. A cultured State will eschew all attempts at conquest, and be as unwilling to tyrannize over another State as to be tyrannized over by one. At the same time, it will always be prepared for war, possessing an army of well-trained, well-armed soldiers, and a well-manned, well-equipped fleet.

Such are the chief features of Aristotle's ideal State, based, as he believes, on man's political nature and the history of the past. Like all social ideals, like heaven itself, as ordinarily conceived, it is a static condition. Its institutions are fixed once for all, and every effort is made to preserve them. It is curious to note in how many points it coincides with Xenophon's ideal.

The purpose of the State is to educate its citizens, to make them virtuous. Virtue is the very life-principle of the State, and it does not depend, as other conditions do, upon nature or chance, but upon free will. The ideal State, like every other, must educate with a view to its own institutions, since only in this way can these be preserved. "And, since the State, as a whole, has but one aim, it is evident that the political education of all the citizens ought to be the same, and that this is a matter for the State to attend to, and not one to be left to individual caprice, as is now almost universally done, when every parent attends to the education of his own children, and gives them whatever schooling suits his own fancy." For the education of those members of the State who are not citizens the State makes no provision. They

learn their practical duties by performing them, and
are completely under the control of the citizens.
Aristotle makes the most vigorous efforts to prove
that slavery has its justification in nature, which has
established between Greek and barbarian the relation
of master and slave (see p. 12). As woman belongs
to the family, and is only indirectly a citizen of the
State, her education is entrusted to the former institution. The daughter is to be educated by the parents, and the wife by the husband, exactly as recommended by Xenophon.

Having concluded that education ought to be a
matter of State legislation, and the same for all the
citizens, he continues: "It remains to inquire what
shall be the nature of the education, and the method
of imparting it. . . . The present state of education
leaves this question in a perfect muddle, no one seem-
ing to know whether we ought to teach those subjects
which enable people to make a living, or those which
foster worth, or, finally, accomplishments. All have
had their advocates. In regard to those studies which
have worth for their aim, there is no general agreement, owing to the fact that different people have
different views as to what kinds of worth are admirable, and consequently differ in regard to the means
to be employed for the cultivation of them. One
point, however, is perfectly clear, viz. that those
useful things which are necessary ought to be taught.
But it is equally clear that a distinction ought to be
made between liberal and illiberal studies, and that
only those useful subjects ought to be taught which
do not turn those learning them into craftsmen. We

ought to look upon every employment, art, or study which contributes to render the bodies, souls, or intellects of free men unfit for the uses and practices of virtue, as a craft. For this reason it is that we call all those arts which lower the condition of the body crafts, and extend the term to the money-making trades, because they preoccupy and degrade the intelligence. As to the liberal arts, to cultivate an acquaintance with them up to a certain point is not illiberal; but any over-devotion to them, with a view to attaining professional skill, is liable to the objections mentioned. It also makes a great difference for what purpose we do or learn a thing. If a man does a thing for his own, for his friends', or for worth's sake, it is not illiberal, whereas if he does it often for the sake of anybody else, he will be held to be doing something mercenary or slavish."

The next and all-important question is, For what end shall the State educate, — for business or for leisure? In answering this, Aristotle breaks entirely away from the old Greek traditions, as well as from Plato, and maintains that, while it must educate for both, yet education for leisure is far more important than education for business, and cites Nature as his authority. "Nature itself demands," he says, "not only that we should pursue business properly, but that we should be able to employ our leisure elegantly. If we must have both, we must; but leisure is preferable to business, and our final inquiry must be, in what sort of employment we shall spend our leisure. It is useless to say that we are to spend it in play, and that play is the end and aim of our life.

If this is impossible, and the truth is that the proper
place for play is in the midst of business (it is the
man who is toiling that requires recreation, which is
the aim of play, business being accompanied with
exertion and tension), then, in having recourse to
play, we must select the proper seasons for adminis-
tering it, just as if it were a medicine. Indeed, all
such movement of the soul is relaxation, and becomes
recreation on account of the pleasure which it affords.
Leisure, on the contrary, is considered, in and by
itself, to involve pleasure, happiness, and a blessed
life. These fall to the lot of those who have leisure,
not of those who are engaged in business. Those
who engage in business do so for some ulterior end
not realized in it, whereas happiness is itself an end
and, according to universal belief, brings, not pain
but pleasure. Of course, as to the nature of this
pleasure, there is at present a variety of opinions,
every one having his own preferences due to his
character and habits, and the highest type of man
preferring the highest type of pleasure and that which
arises from the noblest things. We need no further
argument to show that we should receive instruction
and education in certain things with a view to *otium
cum dignitate* (or cultured leisure), and that these
should be ends in themselves, in contradistinction to
the instruction given for business, which is necessary
and has an ulterior aim."

Three principles Aristotle lays down as valid for
all education: (1) that the training of the body
ought to take precedence in time over that of the
mind; (2) that pupils should be taught to do things

before they are taught the reasons and principles of them; (3) that learning is never playing, or for the sake of playing.

The periods of education distinguished by Aristotle are: (1) Childhood, extending from birth to the end of the seventh year, and spent in healthy growing and, latterly, in preparation for discipline; (2) Boyhood, from the beginning of the eighth year to the advent of puberty, devoted to the lighter forms of discipline, bodily and mental; (3) Youth, from the age of puberty to the end of the twenty-first year, occupied with the severer forms of discipline; (4) Manhood, devoted to State duties. All these are but preparations for the divine life of the soul. We shall treat these in order, including the second and third under one head.

CHAPTER V

EDUCATION DURING THE FIRST SEVEN YEARS

Suffer no lewdness or indecent speech
The apartment of tender youth to reach. — JUVENAL.

Le cœur d'un homme vierge est un vase profond —
Lorsque la première eau qu'on y verse est impure,
La mer y passerait sans laver la souillure;
Car l'abîme est immense, et la tache est au fond.
— ALFRED DE MUSSET.

THE State must begin the education of children before their birth; indeed, before the marriage of their parents. It must see that only persons of robust constitutions marry. Athletes are not suited for marriage; neither are weaklings. The best age for marriage is thirty-seven for a man, and eighteen for a woman. During their pregnancy women must take special care of their health, living on light food, and taking short walks. The State should make a law that they visit the temples of certain gods every day, and offer up a prayer of thanksgiving for the honor conferred upon them. They must carefully avoid all forms of emotional excitement. When defective children are born, they must be exposed or destroyed. The State must determine what number of children each married couple may have, and, if more than this number are begotten, they must be destroyed either before or after birth. "As soon as children are born, it ought to be
184

remembered that their future strength will depend greatly upon the nourishment supplied to them." A milk diet is best, and wine must be avoided. "It is likewise of great importance that children should make those motions that are appropriate to their stage of development. . . . Whatever it is possible to inure children to, they ought to be subjected to from the very outset, and gradual progress to be made. Children, on account of their high natural warmth, are the proper subjects for inurement to cold. These and other points of the same nature are what ought to be attended to in the first years of the child's life. In the following years, up to the age of five, while children ought not to be subjected to any instruction or severe discipline, for fear of impeding their growth, they ought to take such exercises as shall guard their bodies from sluggishness. This may be secured by other forms of activity as well as by play. Care must be taken that their games shall be neither unrefined, laborious, nor languid. As to the conversation and stories which children are to hear, that is a matter for the attention of those officers called Guardians of Public Instruction. It ought to be seen to that all such things tend to pave the way for future avocations. Hence all games ought to be types of future studies. As to the screaming and crying of children, they are things that ought not to be prohibited, as they are in some places. They contribute to the growth of the body, by acting as a sort of gymnastics. Just as persons engaged in hard work increase their strength by holding their breath, so children increase theirs by screaming. It is the business of the Guardians of Public Instruction to provide for their amusement generally, as well as to see that these bring them as little as possible in contact with slaves. It is, of course, natural that at this age they should learn improprieties of speech and manner from what they hear and see. As to foul language, it ought, of course, like everything else that is foul, to be prohibited in all society (for frivolous impurity of talk easily leads to impurity of action), but above all, in the society of the young, so that they may neither hear nor utter any such thing. If any child be caught uttering or doing anything that is forbidden, if he be freeborn and under the age when children are allowed to come to the public table, he ought to be disgraced and subjected to corporal punishment; if he be older, it will be sufficent to punish him with disgrace, like a slave, for having behaved like one. And if we thus prohibit all mention of improper things, with stronger reason shall we prohibit all looking at improper pictures and listening to improper narratives. It ought to be made the business of the Guardians of Public Instruction to see that there does not exist a statue or a picture representing any such thing anywhere in the State, except in the temples of those gods to whom ordinary belief ascribes a certain wantonness. . . . There ought to be a regulation forbidding young persons to be present at lampoons or comedies before they reach the age when they are allowed to come to the public table and partake of wine, and when education has fortified them against all possible danger from them. . . . We all have a preference for what we first know; for this reason everything that savors of meanness or ignobility ought to be made alien to children. From the completion of their fifth year to that of their seventh, children ought to be present at the giving of the various kinds of instruction which they will afterwards have to acquire."

In this brief sketch of primary education we see that Aristotle does not depart far from the notions of Plato. It contains even the revolting features of his scheme. It assumes that the citizens — men, women, and, after a certain age, children — eat at public tables, and that education is entirely managed by the State, — the family, in this respect, being merely its agent. Some of its features, including the Guardians of Public Instruction (παιδονόμοι, child-herds) are plainly borrowed from Sparta.

CHAPTER VI

THE YEARS FROM SEVEN TO TWENTY-ONE

The natures that give evidence of being the noblest are just those that most require education. — SOCRATES.

> We found ourselves beneath a noble castle
> > Encompassed seven times with lofty walls,
> > Defended round by a fair rivulet.
> O'er this we passed as upon solid earth:
> > Through seven gates I entered with these sages.
> > We came upon a meadow of fresh green. — DANTE.

FOR this period, which Aristotle divides into two (see p. 183) by the advent of puberty, he, in the main, accepts the course of study customary in his time. It consists, he says, of four branches, — "Letters, Gymnastics, Music, and Drawing, the last not being universal." Letters and Drawing are taught because they are useful in the ordinary business of life and for a variety of purposes, and Gymnastics because they foster manliness, whereas the purpose of Music is doubtful."

Of LETTERS Aristotle has not much to say, beyond the fact that they are necessary in the common affairs of life. He champions Homer against Plato, and goes into a long discussion to show the value of the drama. Instead of believing, with Plato, that children should see and hear nothing that would excite their emotions, he maintains that it is only by being properly excited and "purged" that these can be trained and made subordinate to the reason. Among the passions that obstruct the exercise of reason are fear and pity. Tragedy rouses these and then drains them off in a pleasant and harmless way. Comedy does the same thing for pleasure and laughter. In fact, he maintains that the special function of the fine arts is to act as cathartics for the different passions. Art is ideal experience. Aristotle has left us a work on tragedy that holds the place of honor in the literature of that subject even at the present day.

DRAWING Aristotle recommends as a branch of study which develops taste and judgment in regard to the products of industrial art; but he says it should not be studied merely for its use in enabling us to choose these, or even works of fine art, correctly, but rather because it enables us to appreciate beauty of form. He adds: "The perpetual demand for what is merely useful is anything but a mark of breadth or liberality."

After thus briefly dismissing Letters and Drawing, Aristotle passes on to Gymnastics and Music, and devotes considerable space to each.

Alongside GYMNASTICS, but distinguished from them, he names PHYSICAL CULTURE (παιδοτριβική), saying that, while the former gives character to the acts of the body, the latter gives character to the body itself. The aim of gymnastic training should be neither athleticism nor ferocity, such as the Lacedæmonians cultivate in their children in the hope of making them courageous. The former is detrimental to the beauty and growth of the body; the latter misses its aim (see p. 41). "Hence nobility, and not ferocity, ought to play the principal part among our aims in physical education. For neither a wolf nor any other wild beast ever braved a noble danger. To do that takes a noble man; and those who allow their children to go too deep into such wild exercises, and so leave them uninstructed in the necessary branches, make them, in point of fact, mere professionals, useful for the ends of the State only in a single requisite, and, as we have shown, inferior to others even in that.

"There is a general agreement, then, as to the utility of Gymnastics and to the manner in which they ought to be conducted. Up to the age of puberty, children ought to be subjected only to the lighter exercises, and all forced dieting and violent exertions eschewed, so that no obstacle may be put to the growth of the body. It is no slight evidence of the fact that violent exercise impedes growth, that there are not more than two or three examples on record of persons' having been victorious at the Olympic games both as boys and men. The explanation of this is, that the others were robbed of their strength in their boyhood by the training they had to undergo." After the advent of puberty, for a period of three years, the young men are apparently to have very little gymnastics, and to devote themselves assiduously to letters, music, and drawing. The period following this is to be devoted to severe exercise and strict dieting, mental exertion being reduced to a minimum; "for the two kinds of exertion naturally work against each other, bodily exertion impeding the intellect, and intellectual exertion the body."

On Music, as a branch of study, we have almost
a disquisition from the pen of Aristotle. The question that first occupies him is, What is the use of
music? Is it a recreation, an occupation for cultured
leisure, or a gymnastic for the soul? It is all three,
he replies, and would deserve study for the sake of
any one of them. At the same time, its chief value
in education lies in its third use. Music imparts a
mental habit; about that there can be no doubt. For
example, the songs of Olympus "render the soul
enthusiastic, and enthusiasm is an affection of the
soul's habit." Aristotle reasons in this way: Music
is capable of affecting us with all kinds of pleasures
and pains. But moral worth at bottom consists in
finding pleasure in what is noble, and pain in what is
ignoble, that is, in a correct distribution of affection.
But in good music the strains that give pleasure are
attached to the ideas that are noble, and the strains
that give pain to the ideas that are ignoble; hence,
by a natural association, the pleasures and pains
which we find in the music attach themselves to the
ideas which it accompanies. "There is nothing that
we ought to learn and practice so assiduously as the
art of judging correctly and of taking delight in gen-
tlemanly bearing and noble deeds. And apart from
the natural manifestations of the passions themselves,
there is nothing in which we can find anger, gentleness, courage, self-control, and their opposites, as
well as the other moods, so well represented as in
rhythms and songs. This we all know by experience;
for the moods of our souls change when we listen to
such strains. But the practice which we thus receive

from rhythms and songs, in rejoicing and suffering properly, brings us very near being affected in the same way by the realities themselves." Here Aristotle draws a distinction between music, which appeals to the ear, and the arts that appeal to the other senses, or rather to sight; for no art appeals to touch, taste, or smell. In the objects of art that appeal to the eye, we have expressions of passions only in so far as they affect the body, whereas in music we have their direct expression passing from soul to soul. Yet persons are deeply moved by statuary and painting, so much so that young people ought not to be allowed to see such works as those of Pauson. How much more then must they be moved by music! "That they are so is quite plain; for there is such an obvious difference of nature between harmonies that the listeners are affected in entirely different ways by them. By some they are thrown into a kind of mournful or grave mood, *e.g.*, by what is known as the mixed Lydian; by others a sentimental turn is given to their thoughts, for example, by languid harmonies; while there is another kind that especially produces balance of feeling and collectedness. This effect is confined to the Doric harmonies. The Phrygian harmonies rouse enthusiasm. These are correct results arrived at by those thinkers who have devoted their attention to this branch of education, — results based upon actual experience. What is true of harmonies is true also of rhythms. Some of these have a steady, others a mobile, character; of the latter, again, some have coarse, others refined, movements. From all these considerations, it is obvious that music is calculated to impart a certain character to the habit of the soul, whence it follows that it ought to be brought to bear upon children, and instruction given them in it. Musical instruction, indeed, is admirably adapted to their stage of development ; for young people, just because they are young, are not fond of persisting in anything that does not give them pleasure, and music is one of the pleasant things. There seems even to be a certain kinship between harmonies and rhythms [and the soul]; whence many philosophers hold that the soul is a harmony, or that it has harmony."

Aristotle, having thus shown that music is a proper subject of instruction, goes on to inquire "whether children ought, or ought not, to be taught music, by being taught to sing and play themselves?" His answer is well worth quoting at full length. "It is quite evident," he says, "that music will have a very much greater effect in moulding people, if they take part in the performance themselves. Indeed, it is difficult, or even impossible, for those who do not learn to do things themselves to be good judges of them when they are done. At the same time, children must have some amusement, and we may look upon Archytas' rattle, which they give to children to spend their energies upon, and to prevent them from breaking things about the house, as a good invention. It is useless to try to keep a young creature quiet, and, just as the rattle is the proper thing for babies, so musical instruction is the proper rattle for older children. It follows that children ought to be taught music by being made to produce it themselves, and it is not difficult to determine either what is suitable

and unsuitable for different ages, or to answer those
people who pretend that the study of music is something ungentlemanly.   In the first place, since people
must, to some extent, learn things themselves, in
order to form a correct judgment about them, they
ought to learn the practice of them while they are
young, so that, when they grow up, they may be able
to dispense with it, and yet, through their early
studies, be able to judge of them correctly and take
the proper delight in them.   To the objections which
some people raise, that music turns people into craftsmen, it is not hard to find an answer, if we consider to
what extent the practice of music ought to be required
of children who are being reared in the civic virtues,
what songs and rhythms they ought to learn, and
what instruments they ought to use — for this makes a
difference.   Herein lies the solution of the difficulty.
The fact is, there is nothing to prevent certain kinds
of music from accomplishing the end proposed.

"It is, of course, obvious that the acquisition of
music ought not to be allowed to interfere with
future usefulness, to impart an ignoble habit to the
body, or render it unfit for civic duties, — either for
the immediate learning, or the subsequent exercise,
of them.   All the beneficial results of musical education would be attained, if, instead of going into a
laborious practice, such as is required to prepare
people for public exhibitions, if instead of trying to
perform those marvellous feats and *tours de force*
which have lately become popular at public exhibitions, and passed from them into education, the children were to learn just enough to enable them to take

delight in noble songs and rhythms, instead of finding a mere undiscriminating pleasure in anything that calls itself music, as some of the lower animals and the bulk of slaves and children do. If so much be admitted, we need be in no doubt respecting our choice of instruments." Aristotle specially condemns the flute, and tells how it came into use, and how it was afterwards discarded, as exerting an immoral influence. "In the same way were condemned many of the older instruments, as the pectis, the barbitus, and those which tended to produce sensual pleasure in the hearers — also the septangle, the triangle, the sambuca, and all those requiring scientific manipulation." . . . "We would, then, condemn all professional instruction in the nature and use of these instruments. 'Professional' we call all instruction that looks toward public exhibitions. The person who receives this pursues his art, not with a view to his own culture, but to afford a pleasure, and that a vulgar one, to other people. For this reason we hold that such practice is not proper for free men, but savors of meniality and handicraft. The aim, indeed, for which they undertake this task is an ignoble one. For audiences, being vulgar, are wont to change their music, and so react upon the character of the professionals who cater to their tastes, and this again has its influence upon their bodies, on account of the motions which they are obliged to go through."

Since different kinds of music have different effects upon the habit of the soul, Aristotle next inquires what kinds are suitable for education. "We accept," he says, "the classification made by certain philoso-

phers, who divide songs into ethical, practical, and
enthusiastic, assigning to them the different harmonies respectively, and we affirm that music is to be
employed, not for one useful purpose alone, but for
several; *first*, for instruction; *second*, for purgation;
and *third*, for cultured leisure, for relaxation, and
for recreation. It is obvious that all harmonies ought
to be employed, though not all in the same way.
The most ethical (*i.e.* those that most affect the *ethos*
or habit of the soul) must be employed for instruction; the practical and enthusiastic for entertainments by professional performers. For those emotions
which manifest themselves powerfully in some souls
are potentially present in all, with a difference in
degree merely, *e.g.*, pity, fear, and also enthusiasm,
a form of excitement by which certain persons are
very liable to be possessed. If we watch the effects
of the sacred songs, we shall see that those persons
are restored to a normal condition under the influence
of those that solemnize the soul, just as if they had
undergone medical treatment and purgation. The
same thing must happen to all persons predisposed to
pity, fear, or emotion generally, as well as to others
in so far as they allow themselves to come within the
reach of any of these; for them all there must exist
some form or another of purgation and relief accompanied with pleasure. In this way those 'purgative'
songs afford a harmless pleasure, and it is for this
reason that there ought to be a legal enactment to the
effect that performers giving public concerts should
employ such harmonies and such songs. The fact is,
since there are two kinds of public, the one free and

cultivated, the other rude and vulgar, composed of mechanics, laborers, and the like, there must be entertainments and exhibitions to afford pastime to the latter as well as the former. As the souls of these people are, so to speak, perverted from the normal habit, so also among the harmonies there are abnormities, and among songs there are the strained and discolored; and each individual derives pleasure from that which is germane to his nature. For this reason performers must be allowed to produce this kind of music, for the benefit of this portion of the public.

" For the purposes of instruction, as has been said, we must employ ethical songs and the corresponding harmonies. Such a harmony is the Doric, as has already been remarked. We must likewise admit any other species of music that may have approved itself to such persons as have devoted attention to philosophic discussion and musical education. . . . In respect to the Doric harmony, it is universally admitted to be, of all harmonies, the most sedate, expressive of the most manly character. Moreover, since our principle is, that the mean between extremes is desirable and ought to be pursued, and the Doric harmony holds this relation to other harmonies, it follows that Doric songs should be taught to young people in preference to any other. Two things, however, must be kept in view, the practicable and the befitting. I mean that we must discuss what is specially practicable for different people, as well as what is befitting. This, indeed, will depend upon the different periods of life. For example, it would not be easy for persons in the decline of life to sing the intense harmonies; for them nature suggests the languid kinds. For this reason those musicians are right who blame Socrates for having condemned the languid harmonies, as subjects of instruction, on the ground that they were intoxicating. (By this term he did not mean inebriating, in the sense that wine is inebriating, — for wine renders boisterous rather than anything else, — but languid.) The truth is, with an eye to the future, to old age, instruction ought to be given in harmonies and songs of this sort. Moreover, if there is any harmony suitable for youth, as tending to refine as well as to instruct, as is the case notably with the Lydian, it, of course, ought to be adopted. It is clear, then, that there are three distinct things to be considered in reference to education, avoidance of extremes, practicability, and appropriateness."

So much for the four branches of study which, according to Aristotle, ought to compose the curriculum of youth. We have noticed that, in his extant works, he says little about Letters and Drawing. Just what branches the former was supposed to include, he has nowhere told us directly; but I think there can be little doubt that he gave a place to Grammar, Rhetoric (including Poetics), Dialectic, Arithmetic, Geometry, and Astronomy, which, along with Music, make up the Seven Liberal Arts, the *Trivium* and *Quadrivium* of the Middle Ages. This curriculum underwent considerable changes at different times, as we can see from Philo, Teles, Sextus Empiricus, St. Augustine, and others; but in Martianus Capella it returned to its original form, and in this dominated education for a thousand years. We might perhaps draw out Aristotle's programme of secondary education thus: —

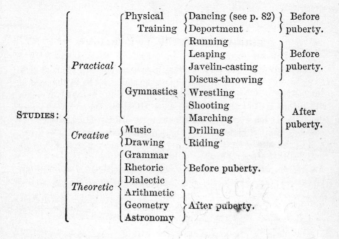

STUDIES:

Practical

Physical Training
  Dancing (see p. 82)
  Deportment
} Before puberty.

Gymnastics
  Running
  Leaping
  Javelin-casting
  Discus-throwing
} Before puberty.
  Wrestling
  Shooting
  Marching
  Drilling
  Riding
} After puberty.

Creative
  Music
  Drawing

Theoretic
  Grammar
  Rhetoric
  Dialectic
} Before puberty.
  Arithmetic
  Geometry
  Astronomy
} After puberty.

CHAPTER VII

EDUCATION AFTER TWENTY-ONE

Be assured that happiness has its source, not in extensive possessions, but in a right disposition of the soul. Even in the case of the body, no one would call it fortunate for being arrayed in splendid garments; but one would do so, if it had health, and were nobly developed, even without such appendages. In the same manner, we ought to ascribe happiness to the soul only when it is cultivated, and to call a man happy only if he possesses such a soul, not if he is splendidly attired outwardly, but has no worth of his own. . . . For those whose souls are ill-conditioned, neither wealth, nor power, nor beauty is a blessing; on the contrary, the more excessive these conditions are, the more widely and deeply do they injure their possessors, being unaccompanied with right-mindedness. — ARISTOTLE.

Zeno used to tell a story about Crates, to this effect: One day Crates was sitting in a shoemaker's shop, reading aloud Aristotle's *Exhortation* (to Philosophy), addressed to Themison, king of the Cyprians, in which the king is reminded that he possesses, in an exceptional degree, all the conditions of philosophy, superabundant wealth, and high position. As he was reading, the shoemaker, without interrupting his sewing, listened to him, until at last Crates said: "Philiscus, I think I will write an *Exhortation* for you; for I see you have more of the conditions of philosophy than Aristotle has enumerated." — TELES.

AT the age of twenty-one, those young men who have successfully completed the State system of training become citizens or politicians, and begin to exercise the functions of such. These are of two kinds, (1) active, practical, or executive, and (2) deliberative, theoretical, or legislative. As action must, on the one hand, be vigorous, and, on the other, guided by deliberation, which requires large experience, the functions of the State must be so arranged that the active duties fall to the young and robust, the deliberative to the elderly and mature. The distinguishing virtue of the former is fortitude, with endurance or patience; that of the latter philosophy. Both equally have self-control and justice. In this way does Aristotle distribute Plato's four cardinal virtues.

When young men first become citizens, they are assigned to posts of active service, civil and military, and thus study practical philosophy — Ethics and Politics — in a practical way. As they grow older, they gradually rise to posts demanding less practice and more thought, until at last they are admitted to the deliberative body, or council, when their active duties cease, and they are able to devote themselves to Speculative Philosophy or Theoretics. These men have now reached the end of life, as far as this world is concerned. They spend their days in cultured leisure, and the contemplation of divine things ($\theta\epsilon\omega\rho\iota\alpha$). The very oldest of them, those who are most conversant with divine things, are chosen as priests, so that they may, as it were, live with the gods, and these be worthily served. Thus gradually, almost insensibly, they pass from the world of time to that of eternity; from the imperfect activity of practice, whose end is beyond itself, to the perfect energy of contemplation, which is self-sufficient and the life of God. In this way Aristotle settles the vexed question with regard to the compatibility and relative value of the practical and the contemplative life.

They are necessary complements of each other. Practice is the realization of what contemplation discovers in the pure energy of God, revealing itself in the world. Thus the practical life of man glides gradually into the contemplative life of God.

Such is the highest view of man's destiny, and the way thither, that the Greeks ever reached, and it is in many ways a most attractive and inspiring one. Its defects are the defects of all that is Greek. They are two: (1) its ideal is intellectual and æsthetic, — a coördinated, harmonious whole, whereof the individual is but a part: not moral or religious — a self-surrender of the individual to the supreme will; consequently, (2) it does not provide for every human being, as such, but only for a small, select number, the fruit of the whole. Its ethics are institutional not personal, and, indeed, the Greek never arrived at a distant conception of personality, that being possible only through the moral consciousness, which is its core. It seeks to find happiness in a correlation and balancing of individual selves, not in the independent conformity of each self to a supreme self. Hence it was that, with all its marvellous grasp and manly prudence, the ideal of Aristotle proved powerless to restore the moral unity of man, until it was absorbed in a higher.

Book IV

THE HELLENISTIC PERIOD
(B.C. 338–A.D. 313)

CHAPTER I

FROM ETHNIC TO COSMOPOLITAN LIFE

'Tis Greece, but living Greece no more. — BYRON.

Most glorious of all the Undying, many-named, girt round with
 awe!
Jove, author of Nature, applying to all things the rudder of law —
Hail! Hail! for it justly rejoices the races whose life is a span
To lift unto Thee their voices — the Author and Framer of Man.
For we are Thy sons; Thou didst give us the symbols of speech at
 our birth,
Alone of the things that live, and mortal move upon earth.
Wherefore Thou shalt find me extolling and ever singing Thy
 praise;
Since Thee the great Universe, rolling on its path round the world,
 obeys: —
Obeys Thee, wherever Thou guidest, and gladly is bound in Thy
 bands,
So great is the power Thou confidest, with strong, invincible hands,
To Thy mighty, ministering servant, the bolt of the thunder, that
 flies,
Two-edged, like a sword and fervent, that is living and never dies.
All nature, in fear and dismay, doth quake in the path of its stroke,
What time Thou preparest the way for the one Word Thy lips have
 spoke,
Which blends with lights smaller and greater, which pervadeth and
 thrilleth all things,
So great is Thy power and Thy nature — in the Universe Highest of
 Kings!
On earth, of all deeds that are done, O God! there is none without
 Thee.
In the holy æther not one, nor one on the face of the sea;
Save the deeds that evil men, driven by their own blind folly, have
 planned;

But things that have grown uneven are made even again by Thy
    hand;
And things unseemly grow seemly, the unfriendly are friendly to
    Thee;
For so good and evil supremely Thou hast blended in one by decree.
For all Thy decree is one ever — a Word that endureth for aye,
Which mortals, rebellious, endeavor to flee from and shun to obey—
Ill-fated, that, worn with proneness for the lordship of goodly things,
Neither hear nor behold, in its Oneness, the law that divinity brings;
Which men with reason obeying, might attain unto glorious life,
No longer aimlessly straying in the paths of ignoble strife.
There are men with a zeal unblest, that are wearied with following
    of fame,
And men, with a baser quest, that are turned to lucre and shame.
There are men, too, that pamper and pleasure the flesh with deli-
    cate stings:
All these desire beyond measure to be other than all these things.
Great Jove, all-giver, dark-clouded, great Lord of the thunderbolt's
    breath!
Deliver the men that are shrouded in ignorance, dismal as death.
O Father! dispel from their souls the darkness, and grant them the
    light
Of Reason, Thy stay, when the whole wide world Thou rulest with
    might,
That we, being honored, may honor Thy name with the music of
    hymns,
Extolling the deeds of the Donor, unceasing, as rightly beseems
Mankind; for no worthier trust is awarded to God or to man
Than forever to glory with justice in the law that endures and is
    One. — CLEANTHES.

THE distinguishing characteristics of Hellenic education were unity, comprehensiveness, proportion,
and aimfulness. It extended to the whole human
being, striving to bring the various elements of his
nature into complete harmony in view of an end.
This end was the State, in which the individual citizen was expected to find a field for all his activities.
We have seen how, while conservative Sparta clung

to this ideal to the last, and rigorously excluded those
influences which tended to undermine it, Athens,
by freely admitting these, gradually broke down the
fair proportion between bodily and mental education,
in an excessive devotion to the latter, and so came to
make a distinction between the man and the citizen.
The result was an epidemic of individualism which
threatened the existence of all that was Hellenic.
Against this destructive power the noblest men in the
nation, an Æschylus, an Aristophanes, a Pericles, a
Socrates, a Xenophon, a Plato, an Aristotle, fought
with all the might of worth and intellect. Some of
them sought once more to remerge the man in the
citizen by means of a despotism and the suppression
of all intellectual pursuits; others, seeing clearly the
impossibility of this, tried so to define the sphere of
the individual that it should not encroach upon that
of the citizen, but stand in harmonious relation to
it. They did this by placing the sphere of the individual above that of the State, and, inasmuch as the
former was a purely intellectual sphere, they found
themselves driven to conclude, and to lay down, that
the contemplative life is the end and consummation of
the practical, that the citizen and the State exist only
for the sake of the individual. They were very far
indeed from seeing all the implications of this conclusion: these showed themselves only in the sequel;
but the fact is, that the principle of the separation
between the man and the citizen, and the assignment
of the place of honor to the former, proved at once
the destroying angel of Hellenism and the animating
spirit of the civilization which took its place. If we

look closely at the schemes of Plato and Aristotle,
we shall see that they try to render innocuous the
spirit of individualism by exhausting its activities in
intellectual relations to the divine, offering it heaven,
if it will only consent to relinquish to the political
spirit its earthly claims. They practically said: Man,
in all his relations to his fellow-men here below, is a
citizen; only in relation to God is he an individual.
The history of the last two thousand years is but a
commentary on this text. From the day when the
master-mind of the Greek world credited man's nature
with a divine element having a supreme activity of
its own, European thought and life have been agitated
by three questions, and largely shaped by the answers
given to them: (1) What is the nature of the divine
element in man? (2) In what form or institution
shall that element find expression and realization?
(3) How shall that institution relate itself to the
State? And they have not yet been definitely
answered.

Principles that are to move the world are never the
result of mere abstract thought, but always of a crisis
or epoch in human affairs. And so it was in the
present case. The separation between the man and
the citizen was accomplished in fact, before it was
formulated in theory. On the other hand, the theory
received emphasis from the events which accompanied
and followed its promulgation. The battle of Chæronea, which took place sixteen years before Aristotle's
death, by putting an end forever to the free civic
life of Greece, removed the very conditions under
which the old ideal could realize itself, and forced

men to seek a sphere of activity, and to form associations, outside of the State. The State, indeed, still maintained a semblance of life, and the old education, with its literature, gymnastics, and music still continued; but the spirit of both was gone. The State was gradually replaced by the philosophic schools, while intellectual training tended more and more to concentrate itself upon rhetoric, that art which enables the individual to shine before his fellows, and to gain wealth or public preferment. From this time on, the spiritual life of Greece found expression in the pretentious, empty individualism of the rhetorician, the lineal descendant of the sophists, and in the philosophical sects, which embodied the spirit of Socrates, their opponent.

The founder of the rhetorical schools may be said to have been Isocrates, who, after being a pupil of Socrates', turned against the philosophic tendency, and championed elegant philistinism. The aim of these schools was to turn out clever men of the world, thoroughly acquainted with popular opinions and motives, and capable of expressing themselves glibly, sententiously, and persuasively on any and every subject. They usually made no profession of imparting profound learning or eliciting philosophic thought: indeed, they despised both; but they did seek to impart such an amount of ordinary knowledge as to place their pupils in the chief current of the popular thought of their time. They thus became the bearers of practical education among a people who, having lost their political life without finding any higher, sought to obtain satisfaction in social intercourse.

For hundreds of years they exerted an enormous influence, and, indeed, at certain times and places were
formidable rivals of the philosophic schools.

The first man of Greek race who attempted to found
a sect or school outside the State was Pythagoras, and
there can be no doubt that all subsequent schools were
in some degree modelled upon his. It is true that
the Pythagorean school had been broken up and dis-
persed long before the days of Plato and Aristotle
(see p. 54); nevertheless, his followers, scattered
over Greece, had carried with them the ideas and
principles of their master, and now that Athens had
fallen into the condition against which the Pythagorean discipline had been a protest, these ideas found
a ready response in the hearts of those men whom the
social life of the time could not satisfy. Hence the
schools of Plato and Aristotle, which had originally
been mere educational institutions, turned, even during the lifetime of the latter, into sects (αἱρέσεις,
heresies, as they were called later on), with definite
sets of non-political principles, in accordance with
which their members tried to shape their lives. It
cannot be said that these two schools were in any high
degree successful, and the reasons were that they were
too purely intellectual, that they made no striking
revolt against political life, and that they called for
a type of man not easy to find. But, shortly after
the death of Aristotle, there arose, almost contem-
poraneously, two other schools, which exerted an
influence, deep and wide, for over six hundred years.
These were the Epicurean and the Stoic. Widely as
these differed in respect to means, they sought the

same end, namely, personal independence, and they
sought it by conformity to laws imposed by no human
legislator, but by nature. The former took the law
of the senses, the latter the law of the spirit, for its
guide; and, by a strange contradiction, while the
former championed free will, the latter professed
fatalism. These four schools were the only ones that
ever met with extensive patronage in Athens, and
with the exception of the Academic, they never
diverged far from the principles of their founders.
In the time of Marcus Aurelius, after Athens had
been for ages a mere Roman university, they were
placed under State patronage, and supported by public
funds, and there is no record to show that this was
discontinued until they were finally closed by the
Emperor Justinian in A.D. 529.

Not long after the death of Aristotle, Athens was
supplanted by Alexandria, as the centre of Greek
influence. Here the rhetorical and philosophic schools
established themselves, and could soon boast a numerous discipleship. This, however, was no longer
exclusively, or even mainly, Greek, but was recruited
from all the nations of the known world, more especially those of the East. Phœnicians, Syrians, Jews,
Persians, etc., not to speak of Egyptians, now became
students of Greek philosophy, and members of philosophic sects, whose members not only studied together,
but often, to a large extent, lived together in com-
munities. About the year B.C. 300 were founded the
famous Museum and Library of Alexandria — the first
university and the first public library in the world.
Round these the various sects gathered, to study, to

discuss, and to exchange opinions. Nor was it Greek thought alone that engaged their attention. The opinions and beliefs of Egypt and the East came in for a share, and, in the end, for the largest share. Nor is this wonderful, when we consider the direction that thought and life were then taking.

We have already seen that, as Greek civic life lost the conditions of its existence, the thoughtful portion of the people came more and more to seek for life-principles in the supersensible world of intellect. The nature of this world Plato and Aristotle had done their best to reveal. But the event proved that neither an ordered host of ideas commanded by the Good, nor a Supreme Intelligence served by a host of lower intelligences, could yield the principles which the life of the time demanded; and thus we find the philosophers of Alexandria striving to people their intelligible world with forms drawn from all the religions of the East, including Judaism. Thus there grew up the various forms of Alexandrine philosophy, compounds of Greek thought and Oriental religion. On the basis of these again were organized, at the same time, various forms of social life, all tending more or less to religious communism. Hence came the Essenes (see p. 59), the Therapeuts, the Neopythagoreans, and the Neoplatonists, all of whom, notwithstanding certain shortcomings, did much to purify life, and to pave the way for a higher civilization.

In B.C. 146, Greece, and, in B.C. 30, Egypt, fell into the hands of the Romans and thenceforth formed provinces of their empire. Athens and Alexandria were now Roman university-towns, while Rome became more and more the diffusing centre of Greek and Oriental influence. It would be impossible, in a work like the present, to give even a sketch of the forms which education assumed in these three great centres, or in the world that revolved round them, in the six hundred and more years that passed between the loss of Greek autonomy and the triumph of Christianity. We shall merely endeavor to give a general notion of its two chief tendencies, which, as we saw, were towards rhetoric and philosophy; and we shall do this in connection with the names of two men, who may be regarded as respectively typical of the two tendencies, Quintilian the rhetorician, and Plotinus the philosopher. By doing so we shall pave the way for the consideration of the Rise of the Christian Schools.

CHAPTER II

QUINTILIAN AND RHETORICAL EDUCATION

Rhetoric is the counterpart of Dialectic. Both have for their subjects those things which, in a certain way, are matters of common knowledge, and belong to no definite science. Hence everybody, in some degree, is gifted with them; for everybody, to some extent, tries to examine and sustain an argument, to defend himself, and to accuse others. — ARISTOTLE.

There is a certain political theory which is made up of many great things. A large and important part of it is artificial eloquence, which they call rhetoric. — CICERO.

Every duty which tends to preserve human relations and human society must be assigned a higher place than any that stops short with knowledge and science. — *Id.*

Zeno, having pressed his fingers together and closed his fist, said that was like Dialectic; having spread them out and opened his hand, he said Eloquence was like his palm there. — *Id.*

To act considerately is of more moment than to think wisely.—*Id.*

I pass to the pleasure of oratorical eloquence, the delight of which one enjoys not at any one moment, but almost every day and every hour. — TACITUS.

Grammar is an experimental knowledge of the usages of language as generally current among poets and prose writers. It is divided into six parts, (1) trained reading with due regard to prosody [*i.e.* aspiration, accentuation, quantity, emphasis, metre, etc.], (2) exposition according to poetic figures [literary criticism], (3) ready statement of dialectical peculiarities and allusions [philology, geography, history, mythology], (4) discovery of etymologies, (5) accurate account of analogies [accidence and syntax], (6) criticism of poetical productions, which is the noblest part of the grammatic art [ethics, politics, strategy, etc.]. — DIONYSIUS THRAX.

214

Reading is the rendering of poetic or prose productions without stumbling or hesitancy. It must be done with due regard to expression, prosody, and pauses. From the expression we learn the merit of the piece, from the prosody the art of the reader, and from the pauses the meaning intended to be conveyed. In this way we read tragedy heroically, comedy conversationally, elegiacs thrillingly, epics sustainedly, lyrics musically, and dirges softly and plaintively. Any reading done without due observance of these rules degrades the merits of the poets and makes the habits of readers ridiculous. — *Id.*

Some arts are common, others liberal. . . . The liberal arts, which some call the logical arts, are astronomy, geometry, music, philosophy, medicine, grammar, rhetoric. — *Scholia to Dionysius Thrax.*

It is obvious that man excels the other animals in worth and speech: Why may we not hold that his worth consists as much in eloquence as in reason? — QUINTILIAN.

The civil man, and he who is truly wise, who does not devote himself to idle disputes, but to the administration of the common-wealth (from which those folks who are called philosophers have farthest withdrawn themselves), will be glad to employ every available oratorical means to reach his ends, having previously settled in his own mind what ends are honorable. — *Id.*

If we count over all the epochs of life, we shall find its pains far more numerous than its pleasures. . . . The first, that of baby-hood, is trying. The baby is hungry; the nurse sends it to sleep: it is thirsty; she washes it: it wants to go to sleep; she takes a rattle and makes a noise. When the child has escaped from the nurse, it is taken hold of by the pedagogue, the physical trainer, the grammar-master, the music-master, the drawing-master. In process of time, there are added the arithmetic-master, the geome-ter, the horse-breaker; he rises early; he has no chance for leisure. He becomes a cadet; again he has to fear the drill-master, the phys-ical trainer, the fencing-master, the gymnasiarch. By all these he is whipt, watched, throttled. He graduates from the cadets at twenty; again he dreads and watches captain and general, etc. — TELES the Stoic (B.C. 260).

The palmy period in the history of Rome is the period when she had no literature. It was only when the Roman nationality began to break up, and cosmopolitan Greek tendencies to lay hold upon the people, that a literature began to appear. For this reason, Roman literature from its very inception is, from absolute necessity, filled with the Greek spirit, and stands in the most direct opposition to the national spirit of the people. — MOMMSEN.

> Quintiliane, vagæ moderator summe juventæ,
> Gloria Romanæ, Quintiliane, togæ. — MARTIAL.

UP to the time when Rome began to decline, the school education of her youth was meagre in the extreme, consisting of reading, writing, and a little law. All later education that was more than this was borrowed from the Greeks. It was about the year 200 B.C., at the close of the Second Punic War, that their influence began clearly to show itself. The severe Cato, who so cordially despised rhetoricians and philosophers, learnt Greek in his old age and wrote, for the use of his son, a series of manuals on ethics, rhetoric, medicine, military science, farming, and law. At the same time Scipio Africanus spent his leisure hours in practising gymnastics. From this time on, and just in proportion as Rome lost her national character and became cosmopolitan, she more and more adopted Greek manners, Greek religion (or irreligion), and Greek education. When, finally, in B.C. 146, Greece became a Roman dependency, it was strictly true that "Captive Greece took captive her rude conqueror." Thousands of Greek schoolmasters, rhetoricians, philosophers, etc., flocked to Rome, and, though attempts were made to expel or suppress them, they held their place, for the simple reason that the education they offered was a necessity of the time. Rome, the mistress of the world, had either to become cosmopolitan or perish, and she preferred the former alternative. She now, for the first time, began to have a literature and to cultivate her own language. The studies which she specially affected were (1) grammar, that is, literature, (2) rhetoric, (3) philosophy, which corresponded to school, college, and university education. The last, like music and geometry, was, for the most part, an elegant accomplishment, rather than a serious study. The physical sciences found little favor.

So long as Roman education was in the hands of Greeks, it was conducted in the Greek language, and the authors read and discussed were Greek. But the Romans, though willing enough to borrow Greek culture, were unwilling to remain permanently in intellectual dependence upon a conquered people, which in many respects they despised. Strong efforts, therefore, were made to develop a national literature and a national education. About the year B.C. 100, Lucius Ælius Præconinus Stilo, a worthy and conservative Roman knight, opened a private class in Latin grammar and rhetoric for young men of the upper ranks, and from this time on the direct influence of the Greeks, except in philosophy, declined. Greek, indeed, continued to be spoken by all persons making any pretensions to culture; but Latin became the language of Roman literature. Among the pupils of Stilo were Varro and Cicero, who, along with Julius Cæsar, may be called the parents of the classical Latin language, literature, and eloquence. Both Varro and Cæsar wrote works on grammar. A certain Cornificius (generally known as *Auctor ad Herennium*) about this time wrote the first Latin treatise on Rhetoric; but

the great authority on the subject, in practice as well
as theory, was Cicero, who wrote no fewer than seven
works on it.   With Cicero's death, and the transformation of the republic into an empire, eloquence lost
its noblest use, the defence of liberty.   Rhetoric,
nevertheless, continued to be cultivated as a fine art
and for forensic use, and, indeed, was made to cover
the whole of the higher education of youth.   Of this
art the most celebrated teacher was Quintilian, "the
supreme director of giddy youth, the glory of the
Roman toga" (*i.e.* civil manhood).

Quintilian was born about A.D. 35 in the Spanish
city of Calagurris (Calahorra), where, later, St. Dom-
inic first saw the light.   He was educated in Rome,
but afterwards returned to his native place and established himself as a teacher of rhetoric.   About A.D. 68,
he was invited by the Emperor Galba to settle in
Rome, which he did, giving instruction in rhetoric
with unparalleled success for twenty years, and drawing a salary from the government.   At the end of that
time, he retired, rich and honored, into private life.
It was after this that he wrote the work which carried
his fame down to posterity, his *Institutio Oratoriae*, or
Education of the Orator.   In the first book of this he
draws out a scheme of preparatory education for the
family and the school; the succeeding ten are devoted
to rhetoric, and the last to the character of the orator,
whom he regards as identical with the cultivated
gentleman.   It is only the first book that concerns
the modern student of education, and of this I shall
now give a brief summary.

The first care of the parent, after the birth of a

child, should be to procure for it a nurse of good moral character and of cultivated speech. A child that early learns bad habits in acting and speaking, rarely, if ever, gets cured of them afterwards. Great care ought to be taken with regard to the child's youthful companions, and to his pedagogue, who ought to be of good character and well-informed. Its first language ought to be Greek ; but Latin ought to be begun early, and both to be carefully cultivated. There is no need to follow the ordinary custom of not allowing the child to learn to read or write before the close of its seventh year. Much can very profitably be done by play long before that. It is a mistake to teach children to repeat the alphabet before they know the forms of the letters. These they may learn from tablets or blocks. As soon as the letters are recognized, they ought to be written. Following with a pen the forms of letters engraved on ivory tablets is a good thing. After letters, syllables must be learnt — all the possible syllables in both languages. After syllables come words, and after words, sentences. In all this process, it is of the utmost importance to secure thoroughness by avoiding haste. The child must not attempt words till he can read and write all the syllables, nor sentences till he is perfectly familiar with words. In reading sentences, he must learn to run ahead, so that, while he is pronouncing one word with his lips, he is recognizing others with his eye. The writing lesson should be utilized in order to make the child acquainted with rare words and good poetry. At this stage, his memory ought to be well exercised, and made to lay up large stores of good literature for future use. At the same time, his organs of speech should be well trained, by being made to pronounce rapidly verses containing difficult combinations of sound.[1]

As soon as he is able, the child should go to school. Home education is objectionable on many accounts, especially for boys intended for orators. These, above all others, must learn sociability, tact, and *esprit de corps*, and form school-friendships. Many moral lessons can be learnt, and many motives employed, in the school, that are not possible in the family. Among the latter is ambition, which "though itself a vice, is the parent of many virtues," and therefore ought to be freely used. Hardly any motive is so powerful.

When a boy is sent to school, his teacher's first business is to investigate his character and capacity. The chief marks of ability are memory and power of imitation. Imitation is not mimicry, which is always a sign of low nature. Slowness, though objectionable, is better than precocity, which should be discouraged in every way. Different treatment is required for different boys: some need the bit, some the spur. The best boy is the one "whom praise excites, whom glory pleases, who cries when he is beaten. Such a one may be nourished with emulation; reproach will sting him; honor will rouse him." Boys ought to have seasons of rest and play, neither too short to afford recreation, nor too long to encourage idleness. Games

[1] Like "Peter Piper," etc., and the German "Messwechsel Wachsmaske."

of question and answer are good for sharpening the wits. In play an excellent opportunity is offered to the teacher for learning the character of his pupils. Corporal punishment is altogether to be deprecated, and, indeed, is unneeded when the teacher does his duty.

What boys learn in school is grammar; but this must be supplemented by music and astronomy. Without the former it will be impossible to scan verse; without the latter, to understand certain allusions and modes of fixing dates in the poets. A little philosophy is necessary for the sake of understanding such poets as Empedocles and Lucretius; geometry, in order to give practice in apodictic reasoning, as well as for practical uses. Thus the curriculum of school education will consist of Grammar, Music, Astronomy, Philosophy, and Geometry.

Grammar consists of two parts, (1) *Methodics*, or the art of correct speaking, (2) *Historics* (German *Realien*), the interpretation of poets, historians, philosophers, etc. *Methodics* — grammar in the modern sense — should aim at enabling a boy to speak and write with correctness, clearness, and elegance. All barbarisms (*i.e.* foreign words and idioms), solecisms, affectations, and careless pronunciations are to be avoided. In the use of language, four things are to be taken into account, (1) reason, (2) antiquity, (3) authority, (4) custom. In reading, the boy must be taught "where to draw his breath, where to divide a verse, where the sense is complete, where it begins, where the voice is to be raised, where lowered, what inflections to use, what is to be uttered slowly, what rapidly,

what forcibly, what gently." "That he may be able
to do all this, he must *understand*. Reading must above
all be manly and grave, with a certain sweetness."
Poetry must not be read either as prose, nor yet in a
sing-song way. All theatrical personification, and
all gesticulation smacking of the comedian, are to be
avoided.

For *Historics* the teacher must be very careful in
his selection of texts. Homer and Virgil are best to
begin with. Though their full import cannot be understood by youth, they awake enthusiasm for what is
noble and spirited, and will often be read in later life.
"Tragedies are useful. There is nourishment in the
lyric poets"; but they must be used with caution and
in selections, from which everything relating to love
must be excluded. Even Horace must be expurgated.
Satire and comedy, though of the utmost value for the
orator, must be deferred till the moral character is
sufficiently established not to be injured by them.
Passages from the poets ought to be committed to
memory. In all reading, the utmost care ought to be
taken to promote purity and manliness (*sanctitas et
virilitas*).

After reading a piece of poetry, boys must be made
to analyze and scan it, to point out peculiarities of
language and rhythm, to enumerate the different mean-
ings of words, to name and explain the various figures
of speech. But far more important than all this it is,
that the teacher should impress on their minds the
importance of systematic arrangement and propriety
of description, "showing what is suitable for each rôle,
what is commendable in thought, what in expression,

where diffuseness is proper, and where brevity." In giving collateral information, whether in history, mythology, or geography, he should keep within bounds, giving only what is necessary and rests on respectable authority. "It is one of the virtues of a schoolmaster to be ignorant of some things."

As regards lessons in composition, the teacher should begin by making his pupils write out from memory the *Fables* of Æsop, in pure, simple, direct, and unadorned language. He should then call upon them to turn poetry into prose, and to paraphrase it, either briefly or diffusely. He should then make them write out proverbs, apophthegms, aphorisms, short, brilliant anecdotes, etc. Famous stories related by the poets may be used as subjects for composition, but chiefly for the sake of information. Beyond this the schoolmaster should not go in the matter of composition. The rest should be left to the rhetorician.

It is of great importance in youthful education that several subjects should be studied at the same time. Boys like and need variety, and, when they get it, it is truly astonishing how much they can accomplish. "There is not the slightest reason for fearing that boys will shrink from the labor of study. No age is less easily fatigued." . . . "Boys are naturally more inclined to hard work than young men."

Such, in brief, is Quintilian's school-programme. It has no place for physical science (except Astronomy), for manual training, or for physical exercise. Play is, indeed, permitted as a necessary recreation, and gymnastics and physical training (παιδοτρίβεια) are recommended in so far as they are necessary to enable

the budding orator to move and to gesticulate grace-
fully; but that is all. "Nothing can please that is
not becoming."

As soon as he is ready, the young aspirant for oratorical fame passes into the hands of the rhetorician,
under whom he learns all the arts, and acquires all
that knowledge, necessary to fit him for his profession.
No kind of knowledge, and no moral excellence ought
to be foreign to the orator. Quintilian is very severe
upon the philosophers for claiming, in their title, to
be, in an exceptional way, lovers of wisdom, and maintains that the true orator is the truly wise and good
man. He is surely superior to the philosopher, who
turns his back upon the world and manifests no interest in human affairs. Moreover, "philosophy may
be simulated; eloquence cannot."

The closing chapter of the last book of Quintilian's
work treats of the orator after his retirement from
public life. He is to devote himself to writing and to
the study of art, science, and philosophy. The picture
is charming; but it ends with death, and there is
nothing beyond. God may be defined for oratorical
purposes; but his existence is a matter of conjecture.

In Quintilian we have the highest type of the civic
man living under a cosmopolitan despotism. His
defects — his pedantry, his servility, his externality,
his worldliness — are only such as are natural to a
good man placed in this position, without any outlook
upon a higher existence.

CHAPTER III

PLOTINUS AND PHILOSOPHIC EDUCATION

The material body, which is subject to motion, change, disso-lution, and division, requires an immaterial principle to hold and bind it together in unity. This principle of unity is the soul. If it were material, it would require another principle of unity, and so on *ad infinitum*, till an immaterial first were reached, which would then be the true soul. — AMMONIUS SACCAS.

Intelligible things, when they are united with other things, are not changed, as corporeal things are when they are united with each other, but remain as they are, and what they are. Soul and body are intimately united, but not mixed. The soul can separate and withdraw itself from the body, not only in sleep, but also in thought. As the sun illuminates and yet remains itself a separate light, so is the soul in its relation to the body. It is not in the body as in place; rather the body is in it and of it. — *Id.*

One's duty is to become first man, then God. — HIEROCLES.

Neither Schelling nor Baader nor Hegel has refuted Plotinus: in many ways he soars above them. — ARTHUR RICHTER.

What is loved by us here is mortal and hurtful. Our love is love for an image, that often turns into its opposite, because what we loved was not truly worthy of love, nor the good which we sought. God alone is the true object of our love. — PLOTINUS.

THE practical and the contemplative lives, which Plato and Aristotle had labored so hard to combine and correlate, in order to save human worth and Greek civilization, fell asunder, despite all their efforts — greatly, of course, to the detriment of both. In the terrible picture which Quintilian draws of Roman life

225

in the first century of our era, we see one side of the
result of this divorce: in the cruel satires of Lucian,
written less than a century later, we may find depicted
the other. But, just as, in the midst of the moral
corruption and brutality, there arose from time to
time worthy men like Quintilian and Tacitus, so amid
the philosophical charlatanry and pretence, there
still survived a few earnest thinkers, who aspired
with all the power that was in them to divine truth,
and strove to find in the eternal world that reality
which was so miserably wanting in this. By far the
greater number of these men were neither Greeks nor
Romans, but Orientals, men whose thinking combined
Greek philosophy with some earnest form of Eastern
mysticism. To such men this life was merely an
opportunity of preparing for a higher, in which lay
all beauty, all good, and all blessedness. It is not
difficult to see what sort of education would follow
from this view of life. It may best be characterized
by the one word "ascetic." It no longer seeks to
train harmoniously all the faculties of body and mind
with a view to a worthy social life, but to enable the
soul to die to the body and to social life, and so rise
to union and consubstantiality with God. In no sect
was this tendency more marked than in the Neoplatonic, or, as it might equally well be called, the
Neoaristotelian or Neopythagorean, the greatest name
in which is Plotinus.

Plotinus was born in Egypt about A.D. 205. His
nationality is unknown. He received his education
in Alexandria — grammar, rhetoric, and philosophy,
— and adopted the teaching of the last as a profession.

He sought in vain, however, for a system that could satisfy him, till he met with Ammonius "the Sack-bearer," whom he at once recognized as his master. This Ammonius had been reared as a Christian, but had apostatized on becoming acquainted with philosophy. His Christian education, however, had not been altogether lost on him; for he had carried over into philosophy a religious spirit, and not a few of the esoteric ideas then current in certain Christian sects. It was this, apparently, that enabled him to give a new direction to philosophy, and to found a new school, whose influence upon subsequent, even Christian, thought, it would be difficult to overestimate. His school was the Neoplatonic, which, more than any other, united profound thought with mystic theosophy ($\theta\epsilon\omega\rho\iota\alpha$).

Plotinus listened to Ammonius for eleven years, and, on the death of the latter, paid a visit to Persia, with the view of studying the religion of that country. He shortly returned, however, and, after a brief sojourn at Antioch, betook himself, in his fortieth year (A.D. 244), to Rome, where he spent the remainder of his life as a teacher of philosophy. His saintly character and his deep, religious thought drew round him a considerable number of earnest men and women, including even members of the imperial family. He made some attempt to found in Campania a Platonopolis, so that his principles might be realized in a social life, in a theosophic community; but this was never carried out. He died in A.D. 270. Plotinus was the only truly great, original ancient thinker after Aristotle.

While Plato and Aristotle had sought to rise to the intelligible world from, and by means of, the sensible, Plotinus, believing that he has attained a direct, intuitional knowledge of the former, sets out from it and thence tries to reach the other. At the summit of being he finds the supreme Platonic principle, the One or the Good, absolutely transcendent and self-sufficient; next below this, the supreme Aristotelian principle, Intelligence or Absolute Knowing, the *locus* of all ideas; and third, the supreme principle of the Stoics, Soul, Life, or Zeus, the animating principle of the world. Good, Intelligence, Life — these are Plotinus' divine trinity, evolved by a process of abstraction from the *Nous* of Aristotle (see p. 161). The members of this trinity are neither personal, conscious, nor equal. Each lower is caused by, but does not emanate from, the next above it; and this causation is due, not to any act of free will, but to an inner necessity. Thus the trinity of Plotinus is a mere energy, acting according to necessary laws. The third member of it turns toward matter, which is mere poverty and hunger for being, and, in so doing, produces a world of gods, dæmons, and mundane beings, the highest of which last is man. All that has matter has multiplicity.

It is easy enough to see what kind of ethics and education will spring from such a system as this. Inasmuch as the good means self-sufficiency, freedom from multiplicity and matter, evil means dependence, multiplicity, materiality. Whatever evil there is in man is due to his connection with matter, for which he is in no sense responsible. His sole business, if he desires blessedness, is to free himself from matter and multiplicity, and return to the unity of the Supreme Good. The steps by which this may be accomplished are, (1) Music or Art, (2) Love, (3) Philosophy or Dialectic: through all these he rises above multiplicity into unity. In all this there is, obviously, neither moral evil nor moral good, and, indeed, the world of Plotinus contains no moral element, for the simple reason that it contains nothing personal, either in God or man. Evil is the product of necessity, and consciousness, implying as it does, multiplicity, is part of it. The unethical character of Plotinus' teaching comes out very clearly in his reversal of the positions of instruction and purgation in the scheme of education. According to the old view, purgation was a mere medical process, preparatory to ethical training (see p. 7). According to the Neoplatonic view, ethical training and the "political virtues" are a mere preparation for purgation and the intellectual virtues. And this is perfectly logical; for evil, being physical, must be cured by physical means. And the means which Plotinus recommends are magical, rather than moral; rites and prayers, rather than heroic deeds; the suppression of the will, rather than its exercise.

Plotinus is too much of a Greek to accept, or even see, all the consequences of his own theory, which makes moral life consist in an attempt to escape from the world and to quench consciousness and personality. Accordingly, though he has a poor opinion of civic life (a thing excusable enough in those days), he believes that the civic virtues ought to be cultivated,

as a means toward the higher, and has apparently
nothing to say against the ordinary grammatical,
rhetorical, and musical education of his time.   He has
a good deal to say in favor of Mathematics, as a preparation for what to him is the supreme branch of
education, Dialectics.   But the tendency of his teaching is only too obvious, and the conclusions which he
did not draw, time and succeeding generations drew
for him.   The effect of Neoplatonism was, in the
long run, to make the super-civic part of man the
whole man, to discredit political life and political
effort, and to pave the way for the mystic, the ascetic,
and the hermit.   Nor were the tendencies of the other
philosophical schools in any marked degree different.
Thus philosophy, instead of contributing to harmonize
man and society, and to restore moral life, came to be
one of the strongest agencies in bringing about confusion and dissolution, by ignoring moral life altogether, embracing superstition, and turning man into
a mere plaything of blind necessity and magical
forces.   And thus ancient civilization fell to pieces,
because man himself had fallen to pieces, and each
piece tried to set itself up for the whole.   The civic
fragment finds its highest expression in Quintilian,
the super-civic in Plotinus.   Ere the fragments can be
united into a truly moral being, a member of a truly
moral society, a new combining force, unknown to
either rhetorician or philosopher, must arise.

CHAPTER IV

CONCLUSION

Truly it was an old world, and even Cæsar's patriotic genius was not enough to make it young again. The dawn does not return till the night has fully set in. — MOMMSEN.

My thoughts are not your thoughts, neither are your ways my ways, saith the Lord. — ISAIAH.

Thou shalt love the Lord thy God with all thy heart, and with all thy soul, and with all thy mind. This is the great and first commandment. And a second like unto it is this, Thou shalt love thy neighbor as thyself. — JESUS.

Render unto Cæsar the things that are Cæsar's, and to God the things that are God's. — Id.

Are not five sparrows sold for two farthings? and not one of them is forgotten in the sight of God. But the very hairs of your head are all numbered. — Id.

We love because he first loved us. If a man say, I love God, and hateth his brother, he is a liar. — JOHN.

By one intelligible form, which is the divine Essence, and one conscious intention, which is the divine Word, things may be known in their multiplicity by God. — THOMAS AQUINAS.

If God acts in all things, and such action in no way derogates from his dignity, but even belongs to his universal and supreme power, he cannot consider it below him, nor does it stain his dignity, if he extend his providence to the individual things of this world. — Id.

Une immense espérance a passé sur la terre. — ALFRED DE MUSSET.

WE have seen that the Greek ideal of life rested upon the complete identification of the man with the citizen. We have seen also how this ideal was paralyzed by the growth of individualism; how the wisest men thought to render this innocuous and even benef icent, by providing for it a sphere of contemplation, superior to that of practice, but organically related to it, and, finally how, with the failure of this attempt, the two sides of human nature, divorced from each other, degenerated, the one into selfish worldliness, the other into equally selfish other-worldliness, both conditions equally destitute of moral significance.

This sad result was mainly due to three causes, (1) that the remedies proposed for individualism were not sufficient, (2) that the best remedy was set aside, (3) that the conditions for which the remedies were offered soon ceased to exist. Both Plato and Aristotle wrote for the small Greek polities, which lost their autonomy through the Macedonian conquest. If it may be doubted whether even the proposals of the latter would have redeemed these polities, had they continued free, it is certain that they would have been ineffective under the changed circumstances. At all events, they were never adopted, and even for the super-civic man the teaching of Plato was preferred to his.

As the new cosmopolitanism deepened the gulf between the citizen and the individual, and immeasurably widened the sphere of the latter, in the same proportion did the teaching of Plato fail to bridge over that gulf, and provide activity for that sphere. To tell the super-civic man now that his function was to contemplate divine things and oracularly deliver laws for the guidance of the world, would have argued an absence of humor not common in those days. Besides, those

persons who claimed to have contemplated divine
things showed no such fitness for legislation as to induce practical men to accept their guidance. The
sober fact was, that the contemplation of divine things,
which more and more absorbed the energy of Greek
thought, was, except for Aristotle, a mere vague aspiration without moral value, and became ever more a
sort of mystic ecstasy, in which the individual, instead
of acquiring insight and power to live worthily and
beneficently in the world, was thrown back upon himself, with his will paralyzed. Nor could this be otherwise, seeing the nature of the divine things, the
contemplation of which was reckoned so important.
Instead of being personal attributes, or a person im-
posing a moral law seen to be binding, they were mere
abstractions, increasing in emptiness the higher they
were in the series, the highest being absolute vacancy.
In vain had Aristotle protested that all reality is individual: the Platonic theory, that all knowledge is
of ideas or universals, prevailed, with the result that
the highest knowledge was held to be knowledge of
that which is absolutely universal, viz. indeterminate
being or, as Plotinus held, something lacking even
the determination of being — the Supreme Good. That
the super-civic man should find satisfaction in gazing
into vacancy, or be any more valuable in the world
after he had done so, no matter how spotless his life
and ecstatic his look, is inconceivable.

But while, in the Greek world, the sphere of activity
of the super-civic man was vanishing into nothing-
ness, among a small and obscure band of restored
exiles of Semitic race, that sphere had come to claim

the entire man and all his relations, practical and spiritual. Isaiah's little band of faithful followers (see p. 133) had grown into a nation, living by no law save that of Jehovah, a very real, very awful, and very holy personality, whom the heaven of heavens could not contain, but who yet watched the rising up and the sitting down of every son of man. Long before Quintilian wrote his elegant treatise on rhetoric, or Plotinus his pantheistic Enneads, there had sprung from the bosom of this people a man who, bursting, at the expense of his life, the narrow bounds of his nationalty, elevated the theocracy of his people into a Kingdom of Heaven, which he bade proclaim to all the world. It was proclaimed, and then (though to some it seemed a stumbling-block, and to others foolishness) the super-civic man, who for hundreds of years had been wandering in darkness, in search of his fatherland, suddenly became aware that he had found it in the Church of Christ. He now no longer tries to escape from the visible world into the emptiness of an abstract first principle; but, in the service of a First Principle who is the most concrete of realities, and who numbers the very hairs of his head, he goes down into the most loathsome depths of the material world to elevate and redeem the meanest of the sons of men. There is no question of bond r free, ruler or ruled, now. In the Kingdom of Heaven there are no such relations. The only greatness recognized there is greatness in service; the only law, the Law of Love. Love! yes, the whole secret is in that one word. By adding love to the conception of the God of his people, by exemplifying it in his own life, and demanding it of his followers, Jesus accomplished what had baffled all the wisdom of the Greek sages. He restored the moral unity of man, abolished the old world, and made a new heaven and a new earth. In vain have the advocates of an indeterminate, self-evolving first principle, whether calling themselves Neoplatonists, mystics, materialists, evolutionists, Hegelians, or Theosophists, striven to bring back the old world with its class distinctions and institutional ethics; in vain have they sought to sink the individual God and man of reality in the universal ideas of thought. The Law of Love, which is the ground of individuality, as well as of true society, has bidden, and will bid them, defiance.

APPENDIX

APPENDIX

APPENDIX

THE SEVEN LIBERAL ARTS

THE Greeks originally recognized two branches of liberal education[1] (1) Gymnastics, for the body, and (2) Music, for the soul. Out of music grew, in process of time, not only the so-called Liberal Arts, that is, the arts that go to constitute the education of every freeman, but also what was regarded as a superfluous luxury (περιττή), Philosophy. It is the purpose of this appendix to trace, as far as possible, this gradual development.

In doing so, one must bear in mind that originally the term "Music" covered, not only what we call music, but also poetry, and that poetry was the vehicle of all the science that then was. The Homeric *aoidos* knows the "works of gods and men." Strictly speaking, therefore, it was out of music and poetry that all the arts and sciences grew. The first step in this direction was taken when Letters were introduced, that is, about the first Olympiad.[2] But it was long before Letters were regarded as a separate branch of education; they were simply a means of recording poetry. Even as late as the time of Plato, Letters are still usually included under Music. In Aristotle, they are recognized as a separate branch. It follows

---

[1] It must be borne in mind that the Greek τέχνη, art, corresponds almost exactly to what we mean by "science." It is defined by Aristotle, *Metaph.*, A. 1; 981 a 5 sqq. Schwegler, in his translation of the *Metaphysics*, renders it by *Wissenschaft*. Ἐπιστήμη is our "philosophy."

[2] See Jebb, *Homer*, pp. 110 sqq.

239

from this that, when we find Greek writers confining soul-education to Music, or Music and Letters, we must not conclude that these signify only playing and singing, reading and writing. Socrates was saying nothing new or paradoxical, when he affirmed that Philosophy was the "highest music." The Pythagoreans had said the same thing before him, and there can be no doubt that Pythagoras himself included under Music (1) Letters, (2) Arithmetic, (3) Geometry, (4) Astronomy, (5) Music, in our sense, and (6) Philosophy (a term invented by him). Plato did the same thing. He speaks of "the true Muse that is accompanied with truth (λόγων) and philosophy." But in his time "Music" was used in two senses, a broad one, in which it included the whole of intellectual education, and a narrow one, in which it is confined to music in the modern sense. It is in this latter sense that it is used by Aristotle, when he makes the intellectual branches of school education (1) Letters, (2) Music, and (3) Drawing. Philosophy he places in a higher grade. Having distinguished Letters from Music, it is natural enough that he should assign to the former the branches which Pythagoras had included under the latter. His literary scheme appears to be (1) Grammar, (2) Rhetoric, (3) Dialectic, (4) Arithmetic, (5) Geometry, (6) Astronomy. Add Music, and we have exactly the Seven Liberal Arts; but, as Drawing must also be added, it is clear that there was, as yet, no thought of fixing definitely the number seven. That Drawing was for a long time part of the school curriculum, is rendered clear by a passage in a work of Teles (B.C. 260) quoted by Stobæus (xcviii, 72), in which it is said that boys study (1) Letters, (2) Music, (3) Drawing; young men, (4) Arithmetic, and (5) Geometry. The last two branches are here already distinguished from Letters; but we cannot be sure that the list is intended to be exhaustive. What is especially noticeable in the list of Teles is, that it draws a clear distinction between the lower and higher studies, a distinction which foreshadows the *Trivium* and *Quadrivium* of later times.[1]

Philosophy, or the highest education, Aristotle divided into (1) Theory and (2) Practice. Theory he subdivided into (a) Theology, First Philosophy, or Wisdom, called later Metaphysics, the science of the Unchangeable, and (b) Physics, the science of the Changeable; Practice into (a) Ethics, including Politics and Œconomics, and (b) Poetics or Æsthetics.

After Teles we hear little of the Greek school-curriculum until about the Christian era. Meanwhile, the Romans, having acquired a smattering of Greek learning, began to draw up a scheme of studies suitable for themselves. It is noticeable that in this scheme there is no such distinction as the Greeks drew between liberal (ἐλευθέριαι, ἐγκύκλιοι, λογικαί) and illiberal (βάναυσοι) arts.[2] As early as the first half of the second century B.C., Cato the Censor wrote a series of manuals for his son on (1) Ethics, (2) Rhetoric, (3) Medicine, (4) Military Science, (5) Farming, (6) Law. It is very significant that the only Greek school-study which appears here is Rhetoric; this the Romans, and notably Cato himself, always studied with great care for practical purposes. It seems that Cato, in order to resist the inroads of Greek education and manners, which he felt to be demoralizing, tried to draw up a characteristically Roman curriculum. Greece, however, in great measure, prevailed, and half a century later we find Varro writing upon most of the subjects in the Greek curriculum: Grammar, Rhetoric, Dialectic,

---

[1] It is a pity that we cannot fix the date of the so-called *Picture* of Cebes (Κέβητος Πίναξ). In this we find enumerated the votaries of False Learning, (1) Poets, (2) Rhetoricians, (3) Dialecticians, (4) Musicians, (5) Arithmeticians, (6) Geometricians, (7) Astrologers (if we count Poets = Grammarians, we have exactly the Seven Liberal Arts), (8) Hedonists, (9) Peripatetics, (10) Critics, "and such others as are like to these." The "Hedonists" (ἡδονικοί) are the Cyrenaics; the "Critics" (κριτικοί) can hardly be the grammarians, though that is usually the meaning of the term in later times. Should we not read κυνικοί?

[2] "Liberal" means fit, "illiberal" unfit, for freemen. The sum of the liberal arts was called Ἐγκυκλιοπαιδεία, which we have corrupted into *Encyclopædia*.

Arithmetic, Geometry, Astronomy, Music, Philosophy, besides many others. He wrote a treatise in nine books, called *Disciplinarum Libri*. Ritschl, in his *Quæstiones Varronianæ*,[1] tried to show that these "Disciplinæ" were the Seven Liberal Arts, *plus* Architecture and Medicine, and Mommsen, in his *Roman History*, has followed him; but Ritschl himself later changed his opinion. There seems no doubt that (1) Grammar, (2) Rhetoric, (3) Dialectic, (4) Music, (5) Geometry, and (6) Architecture were treated in the work: what the rest were we can only guess.[2] There is no ground for the assertion that the Seven Liberal Arts were obtained by dropping Architecture and Medicine from Varro's list. It must have been about the time of Varro, if not earlier, that Roman education came to be divided into three grades, called respectively (1) Grammar, (2) Rhetoric, and (3) Philosophy, the last falling to the lot of but few persons. Of course "Grammar" now came to have a very extensive meaning, as we can see from the definition of it given by Dionysius Thrax, in his grammar, prepared apparently for Roman use (B.C. 90). In the Scholia to that work (I am unable to fix their date), we find the Liberal Arts enumerated as (1) Astronomy, (2) Geometry, (3) Music, (4) Philosophy, (5) Medicine, (6) Grammar, (7) Rhetoric.[3]

But to return to the Greeks. In the works of Philo Judæus, a contemporary of Jesus, we find the Encyclic Arts frequently referred to, and distinguished from Philosophy. The former, he says, are represented by the Egyptian slave Hagar, the latter by Sarah, the lawful wife. One must associate with the Arts before he can find Philosophy fruitful. In no one passage does Philo give a list of the Encyclic Arts. In one place we find enumerated (1) Grammar, (2) Geometry, (3) Music, (4) Rhetoric (*De Cherub.*, § 30); in another

---

[1] Bonn, 1845.

[2] See Boissier, *Étude sur la Vie et les Ouvrages de M. T. Varron*, pp. 332, sqq.

[3] See Bekker's *Anecdota Græca*, ii., 655.

(1) Grammar, (2) Geometry, (3) "the entire music of encyclic instruction" (*De Agricult.*, § 4); in another (1) Grammar, (2) Music, (3) Geometry, (4) Rhetoric, (5) Dialectic (*De Congressu Quær. Erud. Grat.*, § 5); in another, (1) Grammar, (2) Arithmetic, (3) Geometry, (4) Music, (5) Rhetoric (*De Somniis*, § 35), etc.

It would seem that the Encyclic Arts, according to Philo, were (1) Grammar, (2) Rhetoric, (3) Dialectic, (4) Arithmetic, (5) Geometry, (6) Music. Astronomy appears in none of the lists. Philosophy is divided into (1) Physics, (2) Logic, (3) Ethics (*De Mutat. Nom.*, § 10), a division that was long current.

From what has been adduced, I think we may fairly conclude that at the Christian era no definite number had been fixed for the liberal arts either at Athens, Alexandria, or Rome. The list apparently differed in different places. Clearly the Roman programme was quite different from the Greek. Shortly after this era, we find Seneca (who died A.D. 65) giving the liberal arts, *liberalia studia*, as (1) Grammar, (2) Music, (3) Geometry, (4) Arithmetic, (5) Astronomy (*Epist.*, 88). He divides Philosophy into (1) Moral, (2) Natural, (3) Rational, and the last he subdivides into (a) Dialectic and (b) Rhetoric. Above all he places Wisdom, "*Sapientia perfectum bonum est mentis humanæ*" (*Epist.*, 89). Here we see that two of the Seven Liberal Arts are classed under Philosophy. A little later, Quintilian divides all education into (1) Grammar, and (2) Rhetoric, but condescends to allow his young orator to study a little Music, Geometry, and Astronomy.

Turning to the Greeks, we find Sextus Empiricus, who seems to have flourished in Athens and Alexandria toward the end of the second century, writing a great work against the dogmatists or "mathematicians," of whom he finds nine classes, corresponding to six arts, and three sciences of philosophy. The arts are (1) Grammar, (2) Rhetoric, (3) Geometry, (4) Arithmetic, (5) Astronomy, (6) Music : the sciences, (1) Logic, (2) Physics, (3) Ethics. We are now not far from the Seven Liberal Arts; still we have not reached them.

There is not, I think, any noteworthy list of the liberal arts to be found in any ancient author after Sextus, till we come to St. Augustine. In his *Retractiones*, written about 425, he tells us (I, 6) that in his youth he undertook to write *Disciplinarum Libri* (the exact title of Varro's work!), that he finished the book on (1) Grammar, wrote six volumes on (2) Music, and made a beginning with *other five* disciplines, (3) Dialectic, (4) Rhetoric, (5) Geometry, (6) Arithmetic, (7) Philosophy. It has frequently been assumed that we have here, for the first time, the Seven Liberal Arts definitely fixed; but there is nothing whatever in the passage to justify this assumption. The author does not say "*the* other five disciplines," but merely "other five." Among these five, moreover, is named Philosophy, which, though certainly a "discipline," was never, so far as I can discover, called an art, liberal or otherwise. There is not the smallest reason for tracing back the Seven Liberal Arts to St. Augustine, who surely was incapable of any such playing with numbers. He does not, indeed, recognize the "Seven."

It is in the fantastic and superficial work of Martianus Capella, a heathen contemporary of Augustine's, that they first make their appearance, and even there no stress is laid upon their number. They are (1) Grammar, (2) Dialectic, (3) Rhetoric, (4) Geometry, (5) Arithmetic, (6) Astronomy, (7) Music. These, no doubt, were the branches taught in the better schools of the Roman Empire in the fourth and fifth centuries, when, on the whole, the Greek liberal curriculum had supplanted the Roman rhetorical one. There is not the slightest ground for supposing that Capella had anything to do with fixing the curriculum which he celebrates. His work is a wretched production, sufficiently characterized by its title, *The Wedding of Mercury and Philology*. He wrote about seven arts because he found seven to write about.

Attention was first called to the *number* of the arts, and a mystical meaning attached to it, by the Christian senator, Cassiodorus (480–575) in his *De Artibus et Disciplinis Liberalium Litterarum*. He finds it written in Prov. ix, 1, that "Wisdom hath builded her house. She hath hewn out her seven pillars." He concludes that the Seven Liberal Arts are the seven pillars of the house of Wisdom. They correspond also to the days of the week, which are also seven. It is to be observed that he distinguishes the "Arts" from the "Disciplines," or, as they said later, the *Trivium* from the *Quadrivium*. The pious notion of Cassiodorus was worked out by Isidore of Seville (died 636) in his *Etymologiœ*, and by Alcuin (died 804) in his *Grammatica*. Of course, as soon as the number of the arts came to be regarded as fixed by Scripture authority, it became as familiar a fact as the number of the planets or of the days of the week, or indeed, as the number of the elements. About A.D. 820 Hrabanus Maurus (776–856), a pupil of Alcuin's, wrote a work, *De Clericorum Institutione*, in which the phrase *Septem Liberales Artes* is said to occur for the first time. About the same date Theodulfus wrote his allegorical poem *De Septem Liberalibus in quadam Pictura Descriptis*.[1]

The Liberal Studies after St. Augustine did not include Philosophy, which rested upon the Seven Arts, as upon "seven pillars," and was usually divided into (1) Physical, (2) Logical, (3) Ethical.[2] After a time Philosophy came to be an all-embracing term. In a commentary on the *Timœus* of Plato, assigned by Cousin to the twelfth century, we find the following scheme : —

---

[1] I am indebted for a number of these facts to an article by Professor A. F. West, in the *Princeton College Bulletin*, November, 1890.

[2] These terms, which we still find in Isidore and Hrabanus Maurus, are afterwards, in the thirteenth century, replaced by their Latin equivalents: Natural, Rational, and Moral. In the case of the second, this caused considerable confusion, inasmuch as when it ceased to be used as "rational," it took the place of "dialectic."

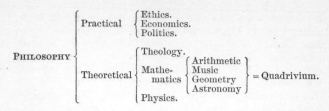

The author expressly says that "Mathematica quadrivium continet"; but he plainly does not include the *Trivium* under Philosophy. This, however, was done in the following century. In the *Itinerarium Mentis in Deum* of St. Bonaventura (1221–74) we find the following arrangements : —

PHILOSOPHY

Natural
{ Metaphysics—essence: leads to First Principle = Father.
Mathematics—numbers, figures: leads to Image = Son.
Physics—natures, powers, diffusions: leads to Gift of Holy Spirit. }

Rational
{ Grammar—power of expression = Father.
Logic—perspicuity in argument = Son.
Rhetoric—skill in persuading = Holy Spirit. }

Moral
{ Monastics—innascibility of Father.
Œconomics—familiarity of Son.
Politics—liberality of Holy Spirit. }

Here we have the *Trivium,* under the division " Rational," while the *Quadrivium* must still be included under " Mathematics." In both cases we get nine sciences or disciplines, and the number was apparently chosen, because it is the square of three, the number of the Holy Trinity. In the latter case this was certainly true. Speaking of the primary divisions of Philosophy, the Saint says: " The first treats of the cause of being, and therefore leads to the Power of the Father ; the second of the ground of understanding, and therefore leads to the Wisdom of the Word ; the third of the order of living, and therefore leads to the goodness of the Holy Spirit."

Dante, in his *Convivio* (II, 14, 15), gives the following scheme, based upon the "ten heavens," nine of which are moved by angels or intelligences, while the last rests in God.

LIBERAL ARTS	Trivium	Grammar..Moon....Angels.
		Dialectic...Mercury.Archangels.
		Rhetoric...Venus....Thrones.
	Quadrivium	Arithmetic.Sun......Dominions.
		Music......Mars.....Virtues.
		Geometry..Jupiter...Principalities.
		Astrology..Saturn...Powers.
PHILOSOPHY		Physics and Metaphysics } Starry Heaven.....Cherubim.
		Moral Science. { Crystalline Heaven } .....Seraphim.[1]
		Theology........Empyrean........God.

In Dante are summed up the ancient and mediæval systems of education.

[1] In the XXVIIIth Canto of the Paradise, these angelic powers are arranged somewhat differently, in deference to Dionysius Areopagita and St. Bernard.

BIBLIOGRAPHY

It is not intended here to give a complete Bibliography of Greek Education, but merely to point the readers of this book, who may desire to pursue the subject further, to the chief sources of information.

1. ANCIENT WORKS

For the first part of the Hellenic Period, that of the "Old Education," our authorities are fragmentary, and often vague. They are the *Iliad* and *Odyssey* of Homer, the *Works and Days* of Hesiod, the fragments of the pre-Socratic philosophers (collected by Mullach, in his *Fragmenta Philosophorum Græcorum*, Paris, Didot, 1860–81, 3 vols. 4to), and the comedies of Aristophanes, especially the *Clouds*. For the second part of the same period, that of the "New Education," the chief authorities are the tragedies of Euripides, the *Clouds* of Aristophanes, the dialogues of Plato, especially the *Protagoras*, *Lysis*, *Republic*, and *Laws*, and the *Cyropædia*, *Œconomics*, and *Constitution of Lacedæmon* of Xenophon.

For Aristotle's educational doctrines, we are confined for information to his own works, and, among these, to the *Ethics* and *Politics*. Of the latter, the closing chapters of the seventh, and the whole of the eighth, book deal professedly with education. Some information may also be gleaned from the recently discovered *Constitution of Athens*.

For the Hellenistic Period, our information is derived chiefly from inscriptions, from the writings of Philo Judæus, Sextus Empiricus, Plutarch (*On the Nurture of Children*), Ælian (*Mis-*

cellanies), Lucian (*Anacharsis* chiefly), Stobæus, Plotinus, Varro, Cicero, Seneca, Quintilian (*Education of the Orator*), Martianus Capella (*Nuptials of Mercury and Philology*), and Cassiodorus, and from stray notices in other poets, historians, and philosophers.

Of the works referred to, these deserve special mention : —

1. Aristophanes, *Clouds*.   Translations by John Hookham Frere, Thomas Mitchell, and W. J. Hickie (in Bohn's Library).

2. Xenophon, *Cyropædia*.   Translation, in *Whole Works translated by Ashley Cooper and Others*, Philadelphia, 1842, and by J. S. Watson and H. Dale (in Bohn's Library).

3. Plato, *Republic*.   Translations by J. Ll. Davies and D. J. Vaughan, by B. Jowett, and by Henry Davis (in Bohn's Library).

4. Plato, *Laws*.   Translations by B. Jowett, and by G. Burges (in Bohn's Library).

5. Aristotle, *Politics* (Books VII, VIII).   Translations by B. Jowett, J. E. C. Welldon, and E. Walford (in Bohn's Library).

6. Plutarch, *On the Nurture of Children*.   Translation in *Morals*, translated from the Greek by several hands, corrected and revised by W. W. Goodwin, Boston, 1878.

7. Quintilian, *Education of an Orator*.   Translation by J. S. Watson (in Bohn's Library).

2. MODERN WORKS

These are very numerous ; but the most comprehensive is Lorenz Grasberger's *Erziehung und Unterricht im klassischen Alterthum, mit besonderer Rücksicht auf die Bedürfnisse der Gegenwart*, Würzburg, 1864–81, 3 vols.   The first volume deals with the physical training of boys, the second with their intellectual training, and the third with the education imparted by the State to young men (ἔφηβοι).   A volume of plates is promised.   The work is badly constructed, but is a mine of information and of references.

Along with this may be named O. H. Jäger, *Die Gymnastik der Hellenen, in ihrem Einfluss auf's gesammte Alterthum und ihrer Bedeutung für die deutsche Gegenwart*, Esslingen, 1850; Fournier, *Sur l'Education et l'Instruction Publiques chez les Grecs*, Berlin, 1833; Becq de Fouquière, *Les Jeux des Anciens*, Paris, 1869; De Pauw, *Recherches Philosophiques sur les Grecs;* Fr. Jacobs, *Ueber die Erziehung der Hellenen zur Sittlichkeit*, Vermischte Schr. Pt. III.; Albert Dumont, *Essai sur l'Ephébie Attique*, Paris, 1875-6; Dittenberger, *De Ephebis Atticis;* Chr. Petersen, *Das Gymnasium der Griechen nach seiner baulichen Einrichtung beschrieben*, Hamburg, 1858; Alexander Kapp, *Platon's Erziehungslehre*, Minden, 1833, and *Aristotle's Staatspædagogik*, Hamm, 1837; J. H. Krause, *Geschichte der Erziehung des Unterrichts und der Bildung bei den Griechen, Etruskern und Römern*, Halle, 1851.

Chapters on ancient education may be found in W. A. Becker's *Charicles* and *Gallus;* in Guhl and Koner's *Life of the Greeks and Romans* — all three translated into English. In *Hellenica* is an essay, by R. S. Nettleship, on the *Theory of Education in the Republic of Plato*, Rivington, 1880, and in Edwin Hatch's *Influence of Greek Ideas upon the Christian Church* (Hibbert Lectures) is a chapter on Greek Education (Lecture II).

INDEX

A

Academics, 112, 210.
Academy, 86, 112.
Achilles, 6.
Æolian Education, 38 *sqq.*
Æolians, 35.
Æschylus, 104 *sqq.*
Æsop's *Fables*, 146, 223.
'Αἶτας, 47.
Alexander the Great, 40, 156 *sq.*, 178.
Alexandria, 211.
Ammonius Saccas, 225, 227.
Amphidromia, 65.
Amyntas, 156.
Anaxagoras, 24, 99 *sq.*
Antisthenes, 112.
Apoxyomenos, the, 82 *n.*
Archytas, 55, 193.
Aristocracy in Athens, 98.
Aristophanes, 105.
Aristotle, Life, 29, 153 *sqq.*
    "   Death, 159.
    "   Philosophy, 161.
    "   Theology, 165.
    "   Theory of the State, 166 *sqq.*
    "   Pedagogical State, 172 *sqq.*
    "   Scheme of Secondary Education, 199.
Arithmetic, how Taught, 77.
Artemis Orthia, 50.
Arts, Origin of, in Greece, 20.
Athenian Education, 60.
Athenian Ideal of the State, 63.
Athletes, 78, 184.
Athletics, 190.

B

Barbarians *vs.* Greeks, 12.
Bodily Training, 77.
Branches of Greek Education, 6.

C

Cæsar, 217.
Cato Major, 216.
Chæronea, Battle of, 157.
Character of the Greeks (Zeller), 18.
Children, Defective, 185.
Children, Treatment of, 185.
Christianity, 233 *sqq.*
Cicero, 217.
Citharist, his Functions, 77.
Citizen, Meaning of, 175.
Clisthenes, 98.
College Education, 85.
Commerce, Effect of, 21, 99 *sq.*
Competition in Education, 71.
Conditions of Education, 9.
Contemplation, 201.
Copernicus, 39.
Cornificius (*Auctor ad Herennium*), 217.
Cretan Education, 42.
Culture-State, 90, 175.
Cynosarges (Gymnasium), 86, 112.
Cyrus, his Education, 115 *sqq.*

D

Dancing, 82 *sqq.*
Democracy in Athens, 92, 99.
Diagogē (διαγωγή), 33, 178.

253

Typography by J. S. Cushing & Co., Boston, U.S.A.

Presswork by Berwick & Smith, Boston, U.S.A.

The Great Educators.

Edited by NICHOLAS MURRAY BUTLER.

"Just in the right time to meet the needs of a large number of teachers who are casting about to find something fundamental and satisfying on the theory of education." — Hon. W. T. HARRIS, *U.S. Commissioner of Education.*

THOMAS and **MATTHEW ARNOLD** and their Influence on English Education. By J. G. FITCH, LL.D., Inspector of Training Colleges in England. *Ready.*

ARISTOTLE and the Ancient Educational Ideals. By THOMAS DAVIDSON, M.A., LL.D. 12mo. $1.00 net. *Ready.*

ALCUIN and the Rise of the Christian Schools. By Prof. ANDREW F. WEST, Princeton. 12mo. $1.00 net. *Ready.*

ABELARD and the Origin and Early History of Universities. By JULES GABRIEL COMPAYRÉ. 12mo. $1.25 net. *Ready.*

LOYOLA and the Educational System of the Jesuits. By Rev. THOMAS HUGHES, S.J. 12mo. $1.00 net. *Ready.*

FROEBEL and Education through Self-Activity. By H. COURT-HOPE BOWEN, University of Cambridge. 12mo. $1.00 net. *Ready.*

HERBART and the Herbartians. By CHARLES DeGARMO, President of Swarthmore College. 12mo. $1.00 net. *Ready.*

HORACE MANN and Public Education in the United States. By Prof. B. A. HINSDALE of the University of Michigan. *Ready.*

ROUSSEAU and Education according to Nature. By Prof. PAUL H. HANUS, Harvard. *In Preparation.*

PESTALOZZI, the Friend and Student of Children. *In Preparation.*

The history of great educators is, from an important point of view, the history of education. These volumes are not only biographies, but concise yet comprehensive accounts of the leading movement in educational thought, and furnish a genetic account of educational history. Ancient education, the rise of the Christian schools, the foundation and growth of universities, and the great modern movements suggested by the names, are adequately described and criticised.

Copies, subject to the privilege of return, will be sent for examination to any Teacher upon receipt of the Net Price.

The price paid for the sample copy will be returned, or a free copy inclosed, upon receipt of an order for TEN *or more copies for introduction.*

Correspondence is invited, and will be cheerfully answered. Catalogue sent free.

CHARLES SCRIBNER'S SONS,

153-157 Fifth Ave., New York.

THE SERIES.

ARISTOTLE.

The whole of ancient pedagogy is Professor Davidson's subject, the course of education being traced up to Aristotle, — an account of whose life and system forms, of course, the main portion of the book, — and down from that great teacher, as well as philosopher, through the decline of ancient civilization. An appendix discusses "The Seven Liberal Arts," and paves the way for the next work in chronological sequence, — Professor West's, on Alcuin. The close relations between Greek education and Greek social and political life are kept constantly in view by Professor Davidson. A special and very attractive feature of the work is the citation, chiefly in English translation, of passages from original sources expressing the spirit of the different theories described.

ALCUIN.

Professor West aims to develop the story of educational institutions in Europe from the beginning of the influence of Christianity on education to the origin of the Universities and the first beginnings of the modern movement. A careful analysis is made of the effects of Greek and Roman thought on the educational theory and practice of the early Christian, and their great system of schools, and its results are studied with care and in detail. The personality of Alcuin enters largely into the story, because of his dominating influence in the movement.

ABELARD.

M. Compayré, the well-known French educationist, has prepared in this volume an account of the origin of the great European Universities that is at once the most scientific and the most interesting in the English language. Naturally the University of Paris is the central figure in the account; and the details of its early organization and influence are fully given. Its connection with the other great universities of the Middle Ages and with modern university movement is clearly pointed out. Abelard, whose system of teaching and disputation was one of the earliest signs of the rising universities, is the typical figure of the movement; and M. Compayré has given a sketch of his character and work, from an entirely new point of view, that is most instructive.

LOYOLA.

This work is a critical and authoritative statement of the educational principles and method adopted in the Society of Jesus, of which the author is a distinguished member. The first part is a sketch, biographical and historical, of the dominant and directing personality of Ignatius, the Founder of the order, and his comrades, and of the establishment and early administrations of the Society. In the second an elaborate analysis of the system of studies is given, beginning with an account of Aquaviva and the *Ratio Studiorum*, and considering, under the general heading of "the formation of the master," courses of literature and philosophy, of divinity and allied sciences, repetition, disputation, and dictation; and under that of "formation of the scholar," symmetry of the courses pursued, the prelection, classic literatures, school management and control, examinations and graduation, grades and courses.

FROEBEL.

Friedrich Froebel stands for the movement known both in Europe and in this country as the New Education, more completely than any other single name. The kindergarten movement, and the whole development of modern methods of teaching, have been largely stimulated by, if not entirely based upon, his philosophical exposition of education. It is not believed that any other account of Froebel and his work is so complete and exhaustive, as the author has for many years been a student of Froebel's principles and methods not only in books, but also in actual practice in the kindergarten. Mr. Bowen is a frequent examiner of kindergartens, of the children in them, and of students who are trained to be kindergarten teachers.

HERBART.

In this book, President DeGarmo has given, for the first time in the English language, a systematic analysis of the Herbartian theory of education, which is now so much studied and discussed in Great Britain and the United States, as well as in Germany. Not only does the volume contain an exposition of the theory as expounded by Herbart himself, but it traces in detail the development of that theory and the additions to it made by such distinguished names as Ziller, Stoy, Frick, Rein, and the American School of Herbartians. Especially valuable will be found Dr. DeGarmo's careful and systematic exposition of the problems that centre around the concentration and correlation of studies. These problems are generally acknowledged to be the most pressing and important at present before the teachers of the country.

3

NOTICES OF THE SERIES.

"Admirably conceived in a truly philosophic spirit and executed with unusual skill. It is rare to find books on pedagogy at once so instructive and so interesting. . . . I hope to read them all, which is more than I can say of any other series." — WILLIAM PRESTON JOHNSTON, *Tulane University*.

"I am very glad to see this excellent contribution to the history of education. Professor Davidson's work is admirable. His topic is one of the most profitable in the entire history of culture." — W. T. HARRIS, *U. S. Commissioner of Education*.

"I have examined with much interest Professor West's work — 'Alcuin and the Rise of the Christian School.' I cannot doubt that the series of 'Great Educators,' under the general editorial supervision of Professor Butler, will be of much value." — GEORGE P. FISHER, *Yale University*.

"The Scribners are rendering an important service to the cause of education in the production of the 'Great Educators Series.'" — *Journal of Education*.

"We have not too many series devoted to the history and the theory of education, and the one represented at the present moment by the two volumes before us promises to take an important place — a leading place — amongst the few we have." — *London Educational Times*.

"'Aristotle' is delightful reading. I know nothing in English that covers the field of Greek Education so well. You will find it very hard to maintain this level in the later works of the Series, but I can wish you nothing better than that you may do so." — G. STANLEY HALL, *Clark University*.

"I have had great pleasure in examining the advance sheets of Davidson's 'Aristotle, and the Ancient Educational Ideals.' It is a book that appeals to the rank and file of teachers, and its reading is sure to give inspiration and pedagogical insight." — WILL S. MONROE, *California*.

"Please forward at once twenty copies of 'Aristotle and the Ancient Educational Ideals,' by Thomas Davidson. It is a great book, and I must give my Senior Class a taste of it before they graduate." — J. C. GREENOUGH, *State Normal School, Westfield, Mass.*

"This volume on St. Ignatius of 'Loyola and the Educational System of the Jesuits,' by the Rev. Thomas Hughes, will probably be welcomed by others besides those specially interested in the theories and methods of education. Written by a member of the Jesuit Society, it comes to us with authority, and presents a complete and well arranged survey of the work of educational development carried out by Ignatius and his followers." — *London Saturday Review*.

"No one, in England or America, is fitted to give a more sympathetic or lucid interpretation of Froebel than Mr. Courthope Bowen. . . . Mr. Bowen's book will be a most important addition to any library, and no student of Froebel can afford to do without it." — KATE DOUGLAS WIGGIN, *New York City*.

"Professor West's 'Alcuin' — a very interesting and scholarly treatment of an attractive and important theme." — EDWARD H. GRIFFIN, *Johns Hopkins University*.

"I take pleasure in saying that 'Alcuin' seems to me to combine careful scholarly investigation with popularity, and condensation with interest of detail, in a truly admirable way." — Professor G. T. LADD, *of Yale*.